EDITOR: LEE JOHNSON

OSPREY MILITARY DESERT STORM SPECIAL 1

LAND POWER
THE COALITION AND IRAQI ARMIES

Text by
TIM RIPLEY

D0992744

Published in 1991 by
Osprey Publishing Ltd
59 Grosvenor Street, London W1X 9DA
© Copyright 1991 Osprey Publishing Ltd

British Library Cataloguing in Publication Data
Ripley, Tim
    Land power. – (Desert storm special v. 1)
    1. Middle East. Gulf War. Military forces
    I. Title   II. Series
    909.0974927082

    ISBN 1-85532-177-7

Filmset by Keyspools Ltd
Printed by Butler & Tanner, London and Frome,
Somerset

Editor's note

For more information on the units mentioned in this
volume see Osprey's Men-at-Arms and Elite series.

Acknowledgements

A number of individuals gave generously of their time
to help make this book possible. Special thanks go to
Bob Morrison, Peter Johnson, David Nicolle and all at
Headquaters UK Land Forces.

Formation diagrams key

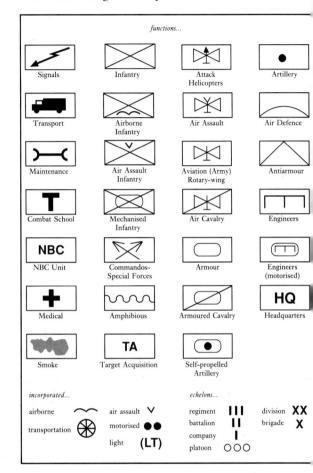

Front cover

US Marines on a live-fire exercise practice for the
assault on Kuwait. They are equipped with M16A2s,
desert camouflage battledress, PASGT body armour
and ALICE webbing. (Military Scene)

INTRODUCTION

During the early hours of 2 August 1990 Iraqi troops launched their invasion of Kuwait. Within hours the United Nations had condemned the unprovoked Iraqi attack and the United States of America started to plan a massive military response. A coalition of 29 states sent forces to support the US effort.

On 17 January 1991 the coalition forces began Operation Desert Storm to liberate Kuwait. This book profiles the land forces involved in the Gulf conflict, looking at their weapons, doctrine, organisation and deployment.

THE INVASION OF KUWAIT

At 2 am on 2 August 1990 Iraqi troops launched their assault on Kuwait. Armoured units and helicopter-borne special forces units led the invasion with attacks on key points throughout the Emirate.

The Iraqi build-up began on 21 July when 30,000 troops started to move towards Kuwait from their peacetime bases around Basra. This was the first stage of the movement of three armoured and four infantry divisions towards Kuwait. By the end of the week the roads from Basra towards Kuwait were jammed with tanks, armoured personnel carriers, artillery and trucks moving south. Giant tented encampments sprang up and artillery emplacements were built. Some 100,000 troops backed by hundreds of T-54, T-55 and T-72 tanks were positioned along the border. Many of them from élite Republican Guard Corps formations. Numerous deception measures were taken by the Iraqis to mask their intentions from Western intelligence services and convince the Kuwaitis that the concentration was only harmless sabre rattling. Important orders were sent

One of the 'All Americans' of the 82nd Airborne covers his squad with his M16A2 while on patrol on the Saudi–Kuwaiti border. He has added his own personal invasion chevrons! (US DoD via Robert F. Dorr)

by despatch riders or telephone land lines and movement of strategic ammunition stocks were kept to a minimum. When the Iraqis struck they took everyone by surprise.

With tactical surprise achieved, the 350 tanks of the leading two Iraqi armoured divisions met no resistance when they crossed the border. The Kuwaiti army had no time to move up to positions on the frontier and could only mount resistance on the outskirts of Kuwait City itself. Heavy fighting took place at Jahre on the main road into Kuwait City from the north. Two Kuwaiti Scorpion light tanks that tried to hold back the invaders were quickly destroyed by Iraqi T-72s. Here the Iraqi deception measures started to work to their disadvantage. The leading armoured units went into battle with hardly any ammunition and they had to halt when resistance was encountered to allow the better-armed Republican Guard units to catch up. Only some 24 T-72 tanks of the Guard carried full ammunition loads. It took until mid-afternoon for the Republican Guard to fight their way through the streets of Kuwait City to the sea front area.

As the main armour drove for Kuwait City artillery fire was brought down on Ali Al Salin airbase to try to prevent Kuwaiti Air Force's Mirage F1CKs from taking off. Some 15 of the Kuwaiti planes

Ankara

TURKEY

Diyarbakir

Tabriz

CYPRUS

Adana

Aleppo

Mosul

Tehran

Nicosia

SYRIA

Kirkuk

Hamadan

IRAN

LEBANON

Samarra

Beirut

Damascus

Isfahan

Haifa

Rutbah

Baghdad

Tel Aviv

Karbala

Kuf

ISRAEL

Amman

Najaf

Amara

Port Said

Jerusalem

IRAQ

Basra

Abadan

Suez

JORDAN

KUWAIT

Shiraz

Aqaba

Kuwait City

Bandar Abbas

Tabuk

Hafar al Batn

EGYPT

Dahran

Manamah

Buraydah

BAHRAIN

QATAR

Hofuf

Doha

Riyadh

Abu Dhabi

Medina

U.A.E.

SAUDI ARABIA

Jidda

Mecca

Taif

Port Sudan

SUDAN

OMAN

Mesewa

Sanaa

YEMEN

ETHIOPIA

Aden

DAVID NICOLLE

DJIBOUTI

SOMALIA

A Challenger MBT advancing at speed throws up a cloud of sand behind it; note the extra track links stored on the front of the vehicle and the protective goggles and scarves worn by the crew. (MoD Army public relations)

however got airborne and attacked the invaders before flying to safety in Bahrain. South of Kuwait City troop-carrying Mi-8 Hip helicopters landed Iraqi commandos in an attempt to take Ahmad Al Jabir airbase, but again the Kuwaiti planes based here managed to escape. Other Iraqi helicopters landed special forces on the strategically important Bubiyan and Warbah islands, which controlled the channels to Iraq's Umm Qsar naval base. A tank column headed for the International Airport and other troops were ordered direct to key points in the city, including the Emir of Kuwait's Dasman Palace. Things however did not go according to plan and the Emir and his close family were able to escape in his armoured Mercedes to safety in Saudi Arabia. Four hours of heavy fighting took place in the grounds of the palace and the Kuwaiti Air Force Headquarters. A number of Iraqi tanks were destroyed in the palace grounds before its defenders, who were trained by the British Special Air Service Regiment, were overwhelmed. The Emir's younger brother, Prince Sheikh Fadh, was killed fighting during this battle. A key target for the Iraqis was the Kuwaiti Central Bank and its massive gold bullion reserves.

The Iraqis soon crushed organised resistance by Kuwait's 20,000 troops, but all over Kuwait City small groups of troops or armed civilians started to launch sporadic attacks on Iraqi units. Behind the combat troops came units of the Iraqi secret police, the feared *Mukhabarat*, who quickly started to round up opponents of the new order. With Kuwait City under Iraqi control, reinforcements now started to flow in from Basra in air-conditioned buses. Three

armoured divisions were dispatched down to the Kuwait-Saudi border to start work building up defensive positions to block any counter attack from the south. Four infantry divisions occupied Kuwait City and secured the lines of communications back into Iraq. Tanks and artillery were dug in along the sea front in Kuwait to counter a seaborne invasion. While the Iraqi troops swiftly crushed the small Kuwaiti Army it seems President Saddam Hussein was not too impressed by his army's performance and a month later he ordered the execution of the Iraqi Chief of Staff Maj.Gen. Abd al-Karim, together with a number of his senior staff officers, who planned the invasion of Kuwait.

Iraq Consolidates

Over the next six months the Iraqis consolidated their forces in Kuwait, or as they termed it Iraq's 19th Province. Some 590,000 troops with 4,200 tanks, 3,000 heavy artillery pieces and 2,600 armoured vehicles were moved into the occupied country or deployed in southern Iraq to support them. The September 1990 peace accord with Iran freed more than 10 divisions to move into Kuwait. The 20-30 Iraqi divisions in the Kuwait theatre of operations were deployed in depth with heavy armoured reserves positioned behind thick frontline defences. Along the Saudi border heavy minefields were sown and giant earthworks (called berms) were built to keep tanks at bay. This outer line was intermingled with barbed wire and booby traps to disrupt infantry attacks. Just behind this line were the main infantry trench and bunker systems, often

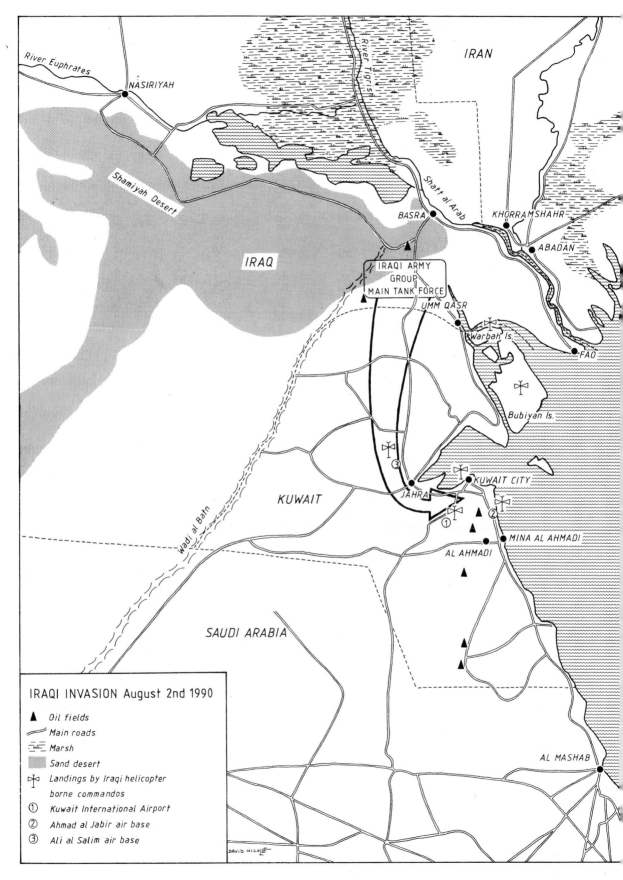

IRAN

River Euphrates

NASIRIYAH

River Tigris

Shamiyah Desert

BASRA

Shatt al Arab

KHORRAMSHAHR

ABADAN

IRAQ

IRAQI ARMY
GROUP
MAIN TANK FORCE

UMM QASR

Warbah Is.

FAO

Bubiyan Is.

③

KUWAIT

JAHRA

KUWAIT CITY

②

①

MINA AL AHMADI

Wadi al Batn

AL AHMADI

SAUDI ARABIA

AL MASHAB

IRAQI INVASION August 2nd 1990

▲ Oil fields
Main roads
Marsh
Sand desert
⚕ Landings by Iraqi helicopter
   borne commandos
① Kuwait International Airport
② Ahmad al Jabir air base
③ Ali al Salim air base

DAVID NICOLLE

formed into triangular earthwork forts. These positions were supported by tanks dug into hull-down firing positions. Some 20 divisions of the Iraqi II, III and VII Corps manned this first echelon position, which extended along the Kuwaiti coast, round along the Saudi–Kuwait border and 50 miles westward into the desert astride the Iraqi–Saudi border. A number of armoured and mechanised brigades were positioned close behind the frontline to be ready to mount local counter attacks. As an added defence against amphibious landings, Chinese-made Silkworm anti-shipping missiles were positioned along the coastline. Mobile SCUD surface-to-surface missile (SSM) batteries were also moved into Kuwait to bring the major coalition bases at Dhahran and Riyadh within range. Backing up the first echelon were at least five independent artillery battalions with long-range 155 mm, 152 mm and 130 mm towed howitzers.

Stretching back to Basra were two more echelons containing the Iraqis' best troops, with the Republican Guard being held in strategic reserve to the south of Basra. In the desert to the west of Kuwait City were six armoured or mechanised divisions who were assigned to the GHQ mobile reserve to counter any breaches in the first echelon defences. Two divisions of this force and two infantry divisions were stationed over the border in Iraq as a flank guard to counter any flanking moves against the exposed western end of the first echelon. The eight Republican Guard divisions were held back as strategic reserve formations to make decisive counter attacks to attempt to turn the land battle in Iraq's favour. Controlling the Kuwait theatre of operations was an army group headquarters located in the Basra area. To support this build-up, huge ammunition dumps were set up all through Kuwait and a number of roads were specially constructed to allow armour to move speedily to threatened sectors of the front. Many dummy positions were also built to confuse coalition aerial reconnaissance.

The Battlefield

The terrain in Kuwait and southern Iraq provided some unusual problems for Iraqi defenders. To the south of Kuwait City along the Gulf coast are a series of salt marshes known as *sabkha*, which are treacherous for heavy armoured vehicles. These are very deceptive and look very firm but have been known to

After rapid shipment to the Gulf, M1A1 tanks are off-loaded from the Cape Mendoc Ino *by a floating crane on to a Saudi dockside. They would shortly be up-armoured by civilians from the Anniston Army depot, Alabama. (US DoD via Tim Ripley)*

swallow up vehicles by the dozen. Stretching out into the desert the going gets distinctly firmer as the sand becomes more gritty. Running along the Kuwait–Iraq border into Saudi Arabia is the Wadi al Batin, a three-mile-wide valley. It is very easy to construct deep field defences in this sand, but on the other hand it is excellent tank country. The desert in Iraq beyond the Wadi is gritty but dotted with rocky outcrops and depressions which turn into small lakes during winter rain storms. Around Basra and along the banks of the Euphrates and Tigris Rivers the terrain becomes very marshy and the few roads are of vital importance for the movement of tanks and other armoured vehicles. Dense palm forests, small lakes and small rivers make this area very unsuitable for tank warfare. North of Basra is the Hawr al-Hammer swamp, which is virtually impassable to large formations of troops. The coastline around Kuwait City features long sandy beaches suitable for amphibious landing craft, but the sea is very shallow and ideal for mines. Around the Fao Peninsular, Bubiyan and Warbah island, open mud flats are common, providing very little cover for defenders or attackers alike. Kuwait City itself is a modern Western-style city with many concrete buildings and industrial complexes which provided ideal cover from aerial reconnaissance.

WAR WITH IRAN

These British Army M109 howitzers are a perfect example of the cutting edge of the coalition's artillery which wrought such havoc with the Iraqi forces.
(Military Scene)

The Iraqi Army that invaded Kuwait was shaped greatly by its eight-year struggle with Iran that ended in stalemate in 1988. It led to the development of Iraq's chemical warfare capability until it became an integrated part of its war fighting doctrine and the growth of the Republican Guard as Iraq's main mobile fighting force.

President Saddam Hussein launched his war against Iran in September 1980 with the objective of capturing the oil-rich region of Khuzistan. The Iranians were still in the midst of their Islamic Revolution and Saddam hoped that the Iranian military would be so enfeebled by Islamic purges that it would put up only token resistance. He couldn't have been more wrong. The Iranians rallied to the defence of their homeland and many of the Shia militiamen of the Iraqi para-military Popular Army deserted in large numbers as soon as they realised that they would have to do some real fighting.

By 1983 the Iranians had gained the upper hand and mounted a series of offensives aimed at pushing into Iraq and deposing Saddam Hussein. They concentrated their efforts on capturing Basra, which, if it had fallen, would have opened up the flat Euphrates plain to the Iranians and allowed them a free run against Baghdad. Using World War I-style infiltration tactics Iranian Revolutionary Guard assault troops broke through Iraqi defences on numerous occasions. Iraqi conscripts manning frontline trench systems surrendered or fled when they found themselves surrounded. Lack of supplies and tank support, however, usually prevented the Iranians from pressing home their advantage to enable them to achieve a decisive victory.

Three years of this type of attack gradually wore the Iraqis down to an extent that in 1986 they had hardly any reserves left to plug the gaps made by the Iranians. By now the Iraqis were getting increasingly desperate. Iran had a population of 54 million compared to Iraq's 18 million, so the Iranian leaders correctly presumed that Iraq would run out of soldiers before Iran if this pattern of warfare continued. To turn the tide, Iraq started to use chemical weapons in massive artillery strikes against poorly defended Iranian infantry. Their main agent was Distilled Mustard (HD), a form of mustard gas which causes instantaneous inflammation of lungs and eyes; later severe blisters appear on the skin. It forms an odourless dust when released into the air and was dubbed 'Dusty Mustard'. It is a non-persistent agent and rapidly dispersed in the desert heat, an important point given that Iraqi troops were as equally ill-prepared to defend themselves against its effects as the Iranians. Indeed, on a number of occasions gas landed on Iraqi positions by mistake causing considerable casualties. Iraqi troops were poorly equipped with chemical warfare protection suits. The few Soviet-supplied suits or locally produced suits were sent only to a few favoured units such as the Republican Guard.

Trusted Iraqi commanders were given *carte blanche* by Saddam to use chemical weapons whenever they thought fit, particularly in situations where Iraqi forces were in danger of being overrun. When the Iranians achieved what seemed like decisive breakthroughs their assault troops would be quickly dowsed in heavy clouds of 'Dusty Mustard' delivered by Iraqi long-range artillery or aircraft. Conventional artillery shells were mixed in with the chemical shells to increase the panic and confusion among the Iranian troops. It was always successful and the Iraqis managed to hold their line together. In 1987 and 1988 they started to use chemical weapons to support offensive operations with some success. Cyanide gas and Tabun (GA) nerve agent was used during these final battles of the war, but they were very difficult weapons to use successfuly. Iraqi troops needed to quickly advance to occupy territory blitzed by chemical weapons before the Iranians had time to recover from the initial shock. The weather had to be perfect to ensure that the chemical agents did not linger and poison Iraqi troops who had advanced into the contaminated area. During this phase of the war the Iraqis carried out their notorious nerve agent attack on the rebel Kurdish town of Halabja, killing some 5,000 civilians. This attack proved very effective in terrorising the Kurds into winding down their revolt.

The Republican Guard

In tandem with the development of Iraq's chemical weapons capability, President Saddam built up an élite armoured corps that was politically reliable and loyal only to him. Regular Army armoured units proved themselves very inept at carrying out complex mechanised operations, so the expansion of the Republican Guard Corps filled this crucial vacuum in the Iraqi ground forces. It was formed first as a brigade-sized formation to protect the Presidential Palace in Baghdad. Its original cadres were recruited exclusively from residents of President Hussein's home town of Tikrit. Their first action was to counter an Iranian breakthrough at Marivan in 1983, but they could only seal the breach not turn back the Iranians. In March 1985, now at divisional strength under the command of Maj.Gen. Talie Khalil Duri, they scored a major victory at Haur al Hawizeh and President Hussein began a large expansion of the

Reminiscent of the Long Range Desert Group of World War II fame, this Land Rover is one of those which helped provide the eyes and ears of the forces assembling in Saudi Arabia. (Military Scene)

Guard to enable them to take the offensive against the Iranians. Their first offensive against the Iranian foothold on the Fao Peninsula in early 1986 ended in dismal failure when the Guards' tanks got stuck in marshy terrain.

By 1986 the Guards had expanded from six mechanised brigades to 17 and totalled some 25,000 highly trained élite troops. They got first choice of all new foreign equipment purchased by the Iraqis. The Guard carried out their most successful and decisive attacks in the spring of 1988 against Fao and the Majnoon Islands. Tank units and special forces units, landed by helicopters, broke the Iranian resistance after the defenders were shelled with chemical weapons. In the Majnoon assault hovercraft were used to carry Guard commando units across marshland.

These attacks broke the back of the Iranian will to continue the war of attrition, and a grateful President showered its commanders and soldiers with honours, extra pay and promotions. The Guard led the Kuwait invasion force because of its political reliability.

Their equipment and training made them a natural choice to fulfil the strategic reserve role in the Kuwait theatre of operations. In August 1990 the Guard Corps fielded eight divisions, four infantry, one mechanised, three armoured. It also had marine and special forces brigades. The armoured divisions, titled *Tarrakalma*, *Medina* and *Hammurabi*, were

British Troops wait on the edge of the tarmac for their transport after arriving in Saudi on the

Kuwaiti Airways 747-200 in the background. (Military Scene)

equipped with 500–600 modern T-72M1 tanks. Around 400 T-55 and T-62 tanks were used by the mechanised and infantry units of the Guard. It had large numbers of South African G-5 155 mm towed artillery pieces and French GCT 155 mm self-propelled howitzers. Anti-aircraft defence was provided by French Roland and Soviet SA-6 surface-to-air missiles. Guard soldiers wore a distinctive small red triangle shoulder patch.

With some 150,000 men under arms, the Guard were mainly political soldiers. They were all volunteers of the Sunni faith. Extra pay, rations and leave ensured their loyalty to Saddam Hussein. The Guard also had its own logistic support system to ensure its independence from the Regular Army. Special units of the Guard were also assigned to Regular Army units to ensure their loyalty to President Hussein and prevent desertions. All senior commanders of Guard units were chosen for their personal loyalty to Saddam. Their commander in January 1991 was Lt.Gen. Ayad al-Rawaii, a veteran of the Iran-Iraq

war, who commanded the final victorious attack on the Fao Peninsula. He had undergone military training in the United States and was considered one of Iraq's best field commanders.

In many ways the Guard were similar to the Nazi Waffen-SS of World War II infamy. In their first years they were very much political soldiers who were primarily concerned with counter-coups against President Hussein's rule. Their lack of conventional military training was reflected in their poor combat performance during the early years of the Iran-Iraq War. Like the Waffen-SS they were expanded and superbly equipped because of their political reliability. It took them many years to master the skills necessary to mount successful mechanised operations. The Guard were very much a law unto themselves and operated outside the normal military chain of command. Their direct links to the President often meant they were ordered to carry out operations for political rather than military reasons and suffered disastrously as a result.

THE IRAQI ARMY

Prior to the invasion of Kuwait the Iraqi army fielded around 50 divisions in its Regular Army, with some 800,000 men under arms. This, of course, excluded men serving with the Republican Guard. Roughly half of the army was deployed along the Syrian–Turkish–Iranian borders to the north of Baghdad. The remainder were positioned along the southern section of the Iraq–Iran border region around Basra. It was from these forces that the bulk of the Kuwait invasion force was drawn. An additional 11 divisions, including two armoured divisions, were formed in August 1990 when the Iraqis recalled over 100,000 reservists. To keep the army up to strength during the Iran-Iraq war few conscripts were allowed to leave the army after completing their two-year period of military service. This practice continued after the end of the war in 1988 and allowed Iraq to maintain its huge ground army.

The civilian trailer on to which this M1 Abrams is ponderously clawing its way is characteristic of the standard method of transporting the armour over any considerable distance. Only once close to the area of operations would Tanks manoeuvre under their own power. (US DoD via Tim Ripley)

The M249E1 Squad Automatic Weapon (SAW) being operated by this paratrooper of the 82nd Airborne was issued before the invasion of Panama, and has now largely replaced the M60 in this role. (US DoD via Robert F. Dorr)

Ordinary soldiers were paid between 80 and 87 dinars a month (about $100 US), but high-ranking professional officers received considerably more along with other fringe benefits.

The highest operational-level formation used by the Iraqis was the army corps, of which there were seven in 1990. Each corps was allocated a number of army divisions and independent brigades depending on their specific task. Corps usually were assigned at least one artillery brigade, a special forces brigade and anti-tank battalions. A number of these types of units were not assigned to corps but were held as central reserve formations by the Armed Forces General Staff (GHQ). The artillery brigade was equipped with towed 130 mm, 152 mm and 155 mm howitzers. They also were assigned multiple rocket launchers.

Chemical weapons were usually allocated to this level of unit. Special forces brigades were equipped with light infantry weapons and were transported by trucks. They were tasked with reconnaissance, harassing operations, air-assault and imposing discipline. Anti-tank units were equipped with wire-guided anti-tank weapons and light armoured vehicles. A large number of anti-aircraft artillery and surface-to-air missiles were assigned to corps-level anti-aircraft units.

Iraq's seven armoured and mechanised divisions mustered around 15,000 men each, organised along the Soviet triangular pattern. With armoured divisions having two armoured brigades and one mechanised infantry brigade. In mechanised divisions there was one armoured brigade and two mechanised infantry brigades. Their artillery regiments usually had 84 towed 122 mm howitzers, with self-propelled artillery being reserved exclusively for the Republican Guard Corps. Armoured and mechanised brigades each fielded four battalions, which were termed regiments in the British fashion. In the better trained divisions all-arms combat groupings were formed at battalion level to conduct specific operations. Tank battalions contained around 40 tanks in three companies, each with four platoons of three tanks. Light armoured vehicles were used as command and support vehicles. Mechanised infantry battalions also used a three-company structure. Each company was made up of three rifle platoons and a weapons platoon. The rifle platoons were made up of three 10-man sections armed with Soviet small arms and RPG-7 anti-tank weapons. Weapons platoons had 82 mm mortars and recoilless rifles or anti-tank guided weapons. Some 40 to 45 armoured personnel carriers and 30 trucks were on strength.

Infantry divisions usually had around 12,000 men

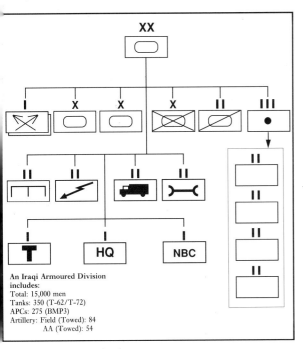

An Iraqi Armoured Division includes:
Total: 15,000 men
Tanks: 350 (T-62/T-72)
APCs: 275 (BMP3)
Artillery: Field (Towed): 84
AA (Towed): 54

Iraqi Armoured Division

formed into three brigades, each with four battalions. Most were very poorly equipped and received the oldest equipment. Hardly any had armoured personnel carriers and they had to rely on trucks for transport. Company and platoon organisation was similar to that in mechanised battalions. Their artillery regiments usually had three battalions of 122 mm towed howitzers.

Supporting the ground forces were almost 500 helicopters of the Army Air Corps. In August 1990 it had 159 armed helicopters, including 40 Soviet-made Mi-24 Hinds, 56 German Bo-105s with HOT missiles, 30 French SA-316s, 13 SA-321s and 20 SA-342 Gazelles armed with HOT. The air corps saw plenty of service during the Iran-Iraq war, and on one occasion a Hind shot down an Iranian F-4 Phantom jet with an anti-tank missile. Soviet-made Hips provide the nucleus of the Iraqi transport helicopter fleet along with assorted French machines.

To defend rear areas and lines of communication the Iraqis developed the para-military Popular Army. More than half of its 850,000 strength was made up of reservists and Ba'ath Party activists who served during weekends and evenings. It was a locally based force with detachments in every city, town and village of Iraq. After its very poor performance in the early days of the Iran-Iraq war, President Saddam restricted its activities to rear areas and only allowed it light arms.

WEAPONS AND EQUIPMENT

Up until the 1980s the Soviet Union was Iraq's main arms supplier, but the pressure of the Iran-Iraq war led the Iraqis to diversify their sources of supply and set up indigenous production facilities for small arms, artillery, all types of ammunition, communications equipment, chemical weapons, and surface-to-surface missiles.

There were four principal types of main battle tanks. Some 500 to 600 T-72M1s served with the Republican Guard. These were mainly of Soviet and Polish origin, although the Iraqis said they had produced their own version called the 'Lion of Babylon'. Over 1,500 Soviet-made T-62s, some with Western laser range finders fitted, served with Republican Guard and the better Regular Army armoured divisions. Soviet T-54/55s and its Chinese-made derivative, the Type 59/69s, were the most numerous tank deployed, with almost 3,000 in service. A number of captured Iranian and Kuwaiti Chieftains, M-47s and M-60s were also in use.

Only around 500 self-propelled (SP) guns were in service, mainly Soviet-made 2S1s and 2S3s. French GCT 155 mm SP guns were also used along with captured Iranian and Kuwaiti M109 155 mm SP guns. The Iraqis manufacture their own version of the Soviet D-30 122 mm towed howitzer. Some 200 South African-made G-5 155 mm howitzers were in service and gave the Iraqis an impressive long-range capability thanks to its extended-range, full-bore, base-bleed (ERFB-BB) ammunition. Soviet M-46 130 mm howitzers with their 27,150-metre range further boosted Iraq's strong artillery force. In total the Iraqis fielded some 3,000 heavy towed artillery pieces, including Austrian 155 mm GH N-45, Soviet 122 mm M1938, 152 mm M1937s and M1943s and Italian 105 mm pack howitzers. More than 200 multiple rocket launchers were in the Iraqi arsenal in August 1990, including Soviet BM-21s and BM-13/16s, Brazilian Astros variants and a number

The Gulf conflict provided the M1A1 Abrams with its first combat deployment, and its performance has confirmed it as one of the outstanding Main Battle Tanks in service in the World today. (Arms Communications)

Gulf War Tank Comparison

	M1A1	Challenger	T-72	T-62	T-55	M60A1
Main armament	120 mm	120 mm	125 mm	115 mm	100 mm	105 mm
Engine	1500 HP	1200 HP	780 HP	700 HP	520 HP	750 BHP
Crew	4	4	3	4	4	4
Max speed on road	67km/h	60km/h	60km/h	50km/h	50km/h	48.28km/h
Weight (kg)	57,150.	62,000	41,000	36,500	36,000	48,987
Fuel capacity (litres)	1,908	1,797	1,000	912	960	1,420

Gulf War Artillery Comparison

	Iraqi			Coalition		
Type	G-5	BM21	2S3	M109A2	M110A2	MLRS
Calibre	155 mm	122 mm Rocket	155 mm	155 mm	203 mm	227 mm
Range	25 miles	12 miles	11 miles	11 miles	13 miles	20 miles (1) 72 miles (2)
Projectile weight	103 lb HE	1,800 lb HE in full salvo	96 lb He	100 lb HE	200 lb HE	(1) 12 × rockets each with 644 M77 bomblets (2) Army Tactical Missile System with 1,000 M74 bomblets in one rocket.

A Challenger tops up with fuel from a Bedford. Even in this oil rich region considerable effort was involved in keeping the armoured formations supplied with their life-blood. (Military Scene)

of home-produced systems. Many of these systems were capable of firing chemical warheads.

Light armoured vehicles came from a variety of sources, but with the Soviet Union being the main source. Elite units were equipped with 1,500 BMP-1/2s while other units made do with some 6,000 inferior vehicles, such as the BTR-50/60, MT-LB, and Chinese YW-531s, Czech OT-62/64s, French Panhard M3s and Brazilian EE-11 Urutus.

Strategic weapons

A large amount of resources were devoted by the Iraqis to the development of strategic missiles and other exotic weaponry. They put great effort into extending the 300 km range of their Soviet-supplied SCUD-B missiles. The 'Al-Hussein' version had a range of 600 km, but to boost its range it could only carry a 500 kg warhead compared to 1,000 kg on the

A Spartan MCT of 7th Brigade churns through the soft sand of the Saudi desert with its missile racks empty, suggesting some unfortunate has been on the receiving end. (MoD Army public relations)

standard SCUD. To extend the range of the 'Al-Abbas' version to 900 km the Iraqis had reduce the warhead to only some 300 kg. A number of SCUD had to be cannibalised to provide the extra fuel tanks and other parts required to construct the Iraqi versions of the missile. Due to the increased length of the 'Al-Hussein' and 'Al-Abbas' missiles they could not be carried on the standard SCUD MAZ-543 transporter-erector-launch (TEL) vehicle so a new one had to be developed. Called the 'Al-Waleed', it was pulled by a Saab Scania tractor unit and resembled a low-loader trailer. The missile was raised into the vertical at the rear of the TEL prior to launch. The Soviets supplied the Iraqis with 36 MAZ-543 TELs, but an unknown number of 'Al-Waleeds' were produced.

During the Iran-Iraq war more than 360 SCUDS were fired at Iran with varying degrees of inaccuracy. They lived up to their reputation for being highly inaccurate with circular error probable (CEP – the size of the area a missile is likely to fall in) of 450 m. Iraqi derivatives of the SCUD were twice as inaccurate and in five tests monitored by the coalition forces in December did not produce CEPs better than 1,000 m. The SCUD and its Iraqi derivatives proved to be a useful terror weapon in the Iran-Iraq war, particularly when the threat of mounting chemical warheads was raised in the later days of the war. No chemical warheads, however, were ever fired at Iran.

The SCUD force was supplemented by shorter-range FROG-7 missiles of Soviet origin and a number of surface-to-air missiles (SAM) converted to surface-to-surface role. A version of the SA-3 Goa was called the 'Barq' and the SA-6 Gainful was called the 'Kser'. Some 50 FROG TELs were supplied to Iraq but numbers of the converted SAMs were not known. The Iraqi missile force was nominally formed into two brigades, but they usually were deployed in small groups of one or two TELs that took their orders direct from the President's headquarters.

One of the more exotic weapons that the Iraqis were producing was the so-called 'Super Gun'. The Canadian artillery designer Dr. Gerald Bull proposed the idea to create a gun on the model of World War I giant artillery. The project foundered when Dr. Bull was assassinated in Brussels in 1990 and British customs officials intercepted parts of one of the barrels. Other products of Dr. Bull did find their way into the Iraqi arsenal thanks to the South African company ARMSCOR. They supplied the Iraqis with G-5 howitzers and the ERFB-BB ammunition which extends the range of Soviet 130 mm howitzers from 27 km to 40 km.

DESERT SHIELD

In the six months following the Iraqi invasion of Kuwait the United States dispatched almost half a million men to the Middle East under the code name Operation Desert Shield. The first wave of forces arrived in Saudi Arabia in August, September and November 1990 with the task of defending the kingdom from further Iraqi aggression. Starting in November an additional 200,000 troops were ordered to the Middle East to give US commanders the option of offensive action to eject the Iraqis from Kuwait.

This unprecedented movement of forces was possible thanks to more than a decade of contingency planning and training by the US armed forces to rapidly deploy combat units to the crisis-torn Middle East. The first moves to enhance US capability for this type of operation were taken by President Jimmy Carter in November 1979 at the height of the Iranian Hostage crisis. He was horrified to learn that apart from US Navy carrier battle groups and the lightly rmed 82nd Airborne Division, few US forces could rapidly intervene in the area. To co-ordinate a possible US intervention he ordered the establishment of the Rapid Deployment Joint Task Force (RDJTF). This multi-service headquarters was responsible for any operations in the Arabian Peninular, Iran, Pakistan, Afghanistan, the Horn of Africa, Egypt and Sudan.

While the Iranian crisis may have been the stimulus for its creation, the Soviet invasion of Afghanistan in December 1979 refocused the RDJTF's efforts at countering Soviet incursion into the Middle East. To practise operating in the Middle East a series of exercises was held with friendly states in the Middle East, such as the 'Bright Star' series in Egypt from November 1990. US Marines of the RDJTF also practised amphibious assaults on beaches in Oman. Agreements were reached with Kenya, Somalia and Pakistan for their ports to be used by US support ships. The former British island of Diego Garcia was transformed into a major base for B-52 bombers, maritime patrol aircraft and a fleet of ships containing weapons, vehicles and equipment for Marine Corps expeditionary brigades.

Of crucial importance to the success of any US intervention in the region was the political and military support of the Gulf states, particularly Saudi Arabia. Military ties were increased with Saudi Arabia and much of the kingdom's military infrastructure was built specially to accommodate a large influx of US aircraft and troops. American vehicles and aircraft support equipment were also pre-positioned in the kingdom. Similar arrangements were made with other Gulf states. The Flagship of the US Navy in the Gulf, the USS *La Salle*, was home ported in Bahrain and the Omani island of Masirah was established as a forward airbase and supply installation.

The RDJTF's preparations gathered momentum throughout the 1980s as more resources were devoted to it by the new US President, Ronald Reagan. In 1983 its importance was considerably increased when it was transformed into Central Command, with its headquarters at MacDill Air Force Base in Florida. As a fully fledged joint command it was put on an equal footing with US commands in Europe and the Pacific in the chain of command. The US Third Army was activated at Fort MacPherson, Georgia, to

The soft powdery sand of the Gulf necessitates almost constant stripping and cleaning of weaponry to keep it operational; a lesson obviously learnt by these RAF crews. (Military Scene)

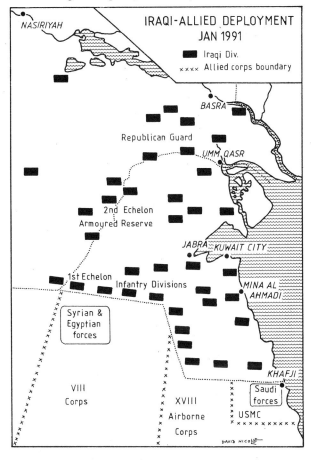

control US Army elements assigned to Central Command. By the mid-1980s the US Army was contributing three full divisions and a number of independent brigades, but in case of emergencies contingency plans were made to draw in other US Army units.

The first elements of any US intervention were to be from the XVIII Airborne Corps and the 82nd Airborne Division based at Fort Bragg, North Carolina. Elements of the 82nd Airborne are kept on immediate readiness to deploy anywhere in the world by USAF transport planes. One parachute company is on two hours' readiness to move, a battalion is on 18 hours notice, and the division's ready brigade, with three paratroop battalions and an artillery battalion, can be airborne in 24 hours. Airmobile troops of the 101st Airborne (Air Assault) Division were also assigned to the corps along with heavy armour of the 24th Infantry Division (Mechanised). After the failure of US special forces operations in Iran and Grenada, the command arrangements for these units were reorganised. They were taken out of the normal army chain of command and special joint service headquarters established at command level. Special Operations Command of Central Command was set up at MacDill with a forward command element on the USS *La Salle*.

Central Command got its first taste of action in 1987 during the so-called Tanker War, when US

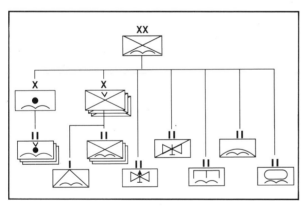

US Airborne Division

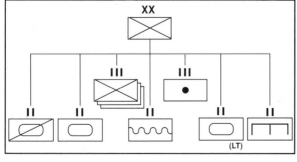

US Marine Corps Division

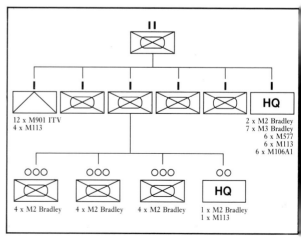

US Mechanised Infantry Battalion

naval and special forces were deployed to protect shipping under Iranian attack in the Persian Gulf and Arabian Sea.

The First Wave

On 3 August 1990 US Defence Secretary Dick Cheney flew to Saudi Arabia and after a three-hour meeting with King Fahd it was agreed that US forces should be dispatched to counter the Iraqi threat. Three days later the 82nd Airborne's readiness brigade was alerted to prepare to move and on 8 August President George Bush announced that he had ordered the division and USAF aircraft to Saudi Arabia.

Hundreds of USAF C-5 Galaxy and C-141 Starlifter transport planes flew into Pope Air Force base near Fort Bragg to collect the 82nd Airborne's 12,790 troops before flying them out to Dhahran airbase in eastern Saudi Arabia. Included in the first contingent was the 'All American' division's light tank battalion, the 3rd Battalion, 73rd Armour Regiment, with some 40 M551A1 Sheridan tanks and the helicopters of the 82nd Aviation Brigade. It mustered some 12 AH-1S Cobras, 43 OH-58Cs, 46 UH-60 Blackhawks and 18 AH-64 Apache attack helicopters. A number of the new Multiple Launch Rocket Systems (MLRS) were quickly flown out to provide the division with added firepower. Patriot surface-to-air missile batteries of the 11th Air Defence Brigade were also flown in to provide air defence around the Dhahran and Jubayl airbases.

This deployment was conducted in a blaze of publicity, but a more covert movement of US Army forces was taking place involving the three battalions of the 5th Special Forces Group, the 160th Special Operations Aviation Brigade and Special Operations Detachment Delta – America's élite anti-terrorist force. These secretive units were quickly hidden away from the world's press in desert bases to prepare for operations deep inside Iraqi-held territory. The 5th SF Group was involved in training members of the Saudi armed forces and the Kuwaiti resistance. Specially modified MH-6 and MH-60 night-flying helicopters of the 160th Brigade carried out intense training in desert flying.

These initial deployments were the first part of a massive deployment plan code-named Operations Plan 90-1002, which envisaged the movement of more than 200,000 men, thousands of armoured vehicles, helicopters, tanks and aircraft to the theatre of operations. Just as important as the combat equipment were hundreds of thousands of tons of ammunition, food and other supplies needed to enable them to sustain their operations. The units involved put pre-prepared contingency plans for mobilising their troops into action, while Central Command dusted off flexible loading plans and movement schedules to match units to available shipping and aircraft. Once the order to execute was given, Operation Desert Shield, as the deployment phase was code-named, quickly moved into high gear.

Air transport was the main means of moving men and urgent supplies to Saudi Arabia and shipping was used for the transport of armoured vehicles, helicopters, ammunition and other heavy items from the continental USA. Most US Army units followed this procedure and were married up with their equipment after it was unloaded from ships in Saudi Arabia in early September and October.

An exception to this procedure were the 1st and 7th US Marine Corps Expeditionary Brigades which arrived in Saudi Arabia in mid-August to meet up with Maritime Prepositioned Ships from Diego Garcia. These ships brought 200 LVTP-7 amphibious armoured troop carriers, 100 M60A1 tanks, six M109 155 mm self-propelled howitzers, six M110 203 mm self-propelled howitzers, 50 towed 155 mm howitzers, aircraft support equipment and enough supplies for 31,000 Marines for 30 days. In an intense 48-hour airlift some 30,000 Marines were flown direct from their bases to meet up with the prepositioned ships and move out into the desert. The arrival of the M60 tanks of the 1st and 3rd Marine Tank Battalions was a particularly welcome addition to the lightly armed airborne soldiers of the 82nd Airborne.

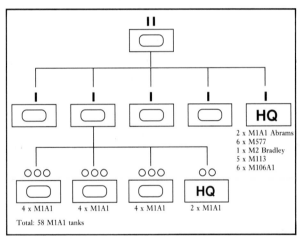

2 x M1A1 Abrams
6 x M577
1 x M2 Bradley
5 x M113
6 x M106A1

4 x M1A1   4 x M1A1   4 x M1A1   2 x M1A1

Total: 58 M1A1 tanks

US Tank Battalion

This remarkable operation effectively trebled U forces on the ground in Saudi Arabia and turned th US ground forces from a meagre trip-wire into credible defensive force. The Marines were justifi ably proud of their achievement and hailed it as vindication of their 'mean and lean' concept of highl mobile, all-arms intervention forces. The Marin units took their integrated air units with them including large numbers of CH-53, CH-46, UH- and AH-1W helicopters, as well as F-18 and AV-8 strike aircraft. Most of these aircraft were drawn from the 2nd and 3rd Marine Air Wings. CH-53 squad rons included HMM 461, 465, 466 and 462. CH-4 squadrons included HMM 165, 263, 161 and 265 AH-1Ws came from 267, 269, 369 and 367. AV-8 Harriers were drawn from VMA-331, 311, 231 an 542. F-18 units included VMFA 333, 451, 314 an 235. To support the on-shore Marine units, amphibi ous forces were positioned in the Persian Gulf aboar assault ships. An Amphibious Task Group centre on the USS *Nassau* had the 4th Marine Expedition ary Brigade embarked. The 2,500-strong 13t Marine Expeditionary Unit was embarked on a tas group led by the USS *Okinawa* and the 26th Marin Expeditionary Unit was embarked on the US *Inchon* task group. These three units all containe integrated air support and helicopter elements.

In the first week of September 1990 ship carrying the equipment and 350 helicopters of th 101st Airborne (Air Assault) Division arrived i Saudi Arabia. The 'Screaming Eagles' specialised i vertical envelopment by helicopter to assault enem

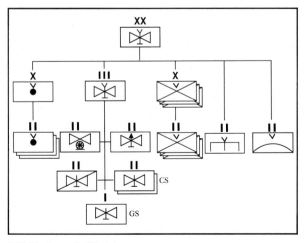

CS

GS

US Air Assault Division

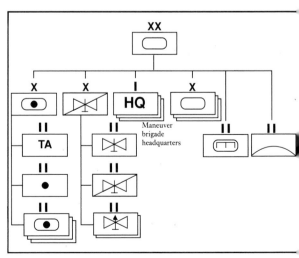

Maneuver brigade headquarters

TA

US Armoured Division

positions or use its strong force of AH-64 Apaches to destroy tank thrusts. Next off the Sea Lift Command fast transport ships were the 290 M1 Abrams tanks and 275 Bradley infantry fighting vehicles of the 24th Infantry Division (Mechanised). Its five tank and five mechanised infantry battalions provided the first modern heavy armour able to take on Iraqi armour on equal terms. The division had recently returned from desert warfare training at the National Training Center at Fort Irwin, California, and was well prepared for operations in the Saudi desert. Only two brigades of the 'Victory Division' took part in the Desert Shield deployment, its National Guard 'roundout' brigade from the Georgia National Guard was left behind and the 197th Infantry Brigade (Mechanised) (Separate) took its place.

The first US unit to deploy the most modern American tanks, the M1A1 Abrams, was the 3rd 'Brave Rifles' Armoured Cavalry Regiment, which took 120 of the tanks with them. US armoured cavalry units are tasked with battlefield reconnaissance and fighting delaying actions and for these missions the Brave Rifles also had 115 M3 Bradleys, 24 M109 self-propelled 155 mm howitzers, 25 AH-1S Cobras, 25 OH-58s and 18 UH-60 Blackhawks.

Early in October the 350 M1 tanks of the 1st Cavalry Division started to arrive to complete the first wave of the US deployment. Like the 24th Division, the 'Cav' had to leave behind their National Guard 'roundout' brigade and took along the 3rd Brigade of the 2nd Armoured Division to bring it up to strength.

The US Army Desert Shield forces were concentrated under the command of the XVIII Airborne Corps, which was able to draw on a number of specialist brigades to boost its combat power. The 18th Aviation Brigade deployed its three helicopter battalions. III Corps Artillery with three field artillery brigades, with M109s, M110s and MLRS, was attached, along with the 'Dragon Corps' own 18th Field Artillery Brigade, which had three battalions of towed 155 mm howitzers. The 12th Combat Aviation Brigade and the 229th Aviation Regiment brought their Apache attack helicopters from Germany. Its arrival in Saudi Arabia brought the total number of US Army helicopters in the Middle East to 950, plus 50 fixed-wing observation and communication aircraft. Medical support was provided by the 7th and 44th Medical Brigades; 525th Military Intelligence Brigade looked after electronic warfare and 35th Signals Brigade provided in-theatre communications. The three battalions of the 16th Military Police Battalions organised a traffic control system and the 20th Engineer Brigade built tented camps and other facilities for US Army units in Saudi

The Engineers are a vital part of any modern military force as this USMC Unimog, digging a defensive trench around one of the Royal Navy's main bases of operation, demonstrates only too well. (Military Scene)

Arabia. Running the huge logistic operation to support Desert Shield were the 1st and 13th Corps Support Commands.

Many US units were dependent on part-time National Guard or Army reserve soldiers to provide key logistic support, particularly water supplies, so on 22 August President Bush authorised the mobilisation of up to 47,000 reservists. Most served in support units in the USA or took the place of active duty servicemen ordered to the Gulf. At this point of the crisis it was not deemed necessary to mobilise reserve combat units, much to the annoyance of the 'roundout' brigades of the 24th Division and 1st Cavalry, who had trained with them in peacetime as part of the Pentagon's Total Force policy.

After the US troops collected their tanks and other equipment from the quayside in Saudi Arabia they moved out into the desert and began a programme of intense training. Thousands of rounds were fired as units practised tactical manoeuvres and fine-tuned their weapons. Army units were mostly concentrated inland from the Dhahran area in reserve positions to counter any Iraqi thrust through Arab units stationed along the Kuwaiti–Saudi border. The two Marine brigades were stationed further north near Jubayl in positions which were more exposed to a surprise Iraqi attack. Before the heavy army divisions arrived in September and October, the US Marines were justifiably nervous and there were numerous 'invasion scares' among their forward troops. On one occasion a Marines CH-53E crashed after frontline US Marines let fly into the night sky with tracer during an alert. The helicopter crew survived the incident, but their machine was riddled with bullet holes and broke in two on impact.

The smooth deployment of such a large US force was largely possible because of a massive support effort laid on by the Saudi government. Unlimited supplies of fuel were made available to US forces; food and water from local sources also reduced the amount required to be shipped in from US stocks and the large number of low-loaders available greatly speeded up the movement of US tank units out into the desert.

Starting on 19 October 1990 the 21st Theatre Area Support Command started to move the first of 750 M1A1 tanks from five storage sites in Germany to railheads before movement by ship to Saudi Arabia. The tanks were valued at $4.8 million and were to be distributed to the 24th Division and 1st Cavalry to replace their older M1s. Some of the M1A1s were also given to Marine tanks battalions to replace their older M60s. Other M1A1s were to be held in storage as casualty replacements. The almost new M1A1s boasted better chemical warfare protection equipment and 120 mm guns.

The Second Wave

To give the US forces in Saudi Arabia the capability to take the offensive against Iraqi forces in Kuwait, President Bush ordered 200,000 additional US service personnel to the Middle East on 8 November 1990. Defence Secretary Dick Cheney also announced that a planned rotation of US troops already in Saudi Arabia would not take place to ensure that the maximum level of forces would be available if the US forces had to take the offensive. The additional US Army units were drawn from bases in Germany and the continental USA. More Marines were also sent and US reserve combat units were mobilised for the first time since the Vietnam War. This deployment lacked the frantic air transport operations that marked the first weeks of Desert Shield deployments in August. Many of the lessons learnt in that period were put to good use to ensure the new units arrived in Saudi Arabia quickly and efficiently. Because of planned defence cutbacks after the collapse of the Berlin Wall some Germany-based tank units were under strength and reinforcements were drafted in from other units to bring them up to battle strength. Before the move to Saudi Arabia they were put through intense firing practice on the Grafenhowhr ranges to build up the team work and gunnery skills of the newly arrived crewmen.

At the centre of new ground force deployment was the US VII Corps from Germany under Lt.Gen. Frederick Franks. Its two armoured divisions, the 1st 'Old Ironsides' and 3rd 'Spearhead Division', were highly trained and well equipped for armoured warfare against the Soviets. Their deployment gave Central Command the armoured punch necessary to take on Iraq's 5,000 tanks on better than equal terms.

The 1st Division, commanded by Maj.Gen. Ronald Griffiths, mustered some 17,000 troops and was equipped with M1A1 tanks and Bradley fighting vehicles. Its six tank battalions and four mechanised infantry battalions were supported by M109s, MLRS and Apache attack helicopters from the two battalions of the 1st Aviation Regiment.

Maj.Gen. Paul Funk commanded the 3rd Armoured Division, which was organised and equipped in a similar way to the 1st Division. It was normally part of V Corps and was only attached to VII Corps for Operation Desert Shield. Part of its aviation brigade, the 229th Aviation Regiment, had already moved to Saudi Arabia as part of the first-wave deployment.

From Fort Riley, Kansas, the 1st Infantry Division (Mechanised) was ordered to link up with VII Corps in Saudi Arabia. The 'Big Red One' was to be augmented by the forward brigade of the 2nd Armoured Division from Garlstedt in Germany with its 120 M1A1 tanks and 50 Bradley infantry fighting vehicles. Maj.Gen. Thomas Rhame's stateside-based units however were only equipped with M1 tanks in five battalions. Two of the division's three mechanised infantry battalions and a tank battalion are normally based in Germany but they were deacti-

The threat posed by the Iraqi Air Force was taken seriously by the coalition and a number of Hawk missile batteries such as *this USMC model were deployed to provide a defensive capability. (MoD Army public relations)*

vated in defence cutbacks and were not considered in a fit condition to be sent to the desert. The division's helicopter assets included an assault company with 15 UH-60s, an attack battalion of AH-1s and AH-64s and a command company with six UH-1s, six OH-58s and three UH-60s.

VII Corps took a strong force of support units with it, including the 17th, 72nd, 210th Field Artillery Brigades equipped with M109s, M110s and MLRS. Engineers from the 7th Engineer Brigade also went with the Corps. The 11th Combat Aviation Brigade shipped out more than 300 helicopters through Rotterdam Docks. Aviation units included the 2/227th, 3/227th, 4/229th Aviation Regts and 2/6th and 5/6th Cavalry with AH-64s. The 236th Medical Company and 6/159th Aviation Regiment took their UH-60As, the 4/159th Aviation Regiment took its UH-1s and OH-58s and the 5/159th took some 24 CH-47 Chinooks. Logistic support for VII Corps was provided by 2nd Support Command.

The 2nd Armoured Cavalry Regiment provided the corps with reconnaissance support; 120 M1A1s, 115 Bradleys, 24 M109s, 25 AH-1Fs, 25 OH-58s and 18 UH-60s manned by 4,500 soldiers.

In addition to dispatching this massive force of active duty units to Saudi Arabia the US Army also mobilised three National Guard brigades in preparation for possible deployment. They were first sent to the Fort Irving National Training Center for intensive training in desert warfare before US military chiefs would decide to deploy them to Saudi Arabia.

'Sherry Lynne' is a Bell AH-IW SuperCobra from Camp Pendleton, California. Packing an M-197 20 mm automatic gun, this is one young lady any Iraqi would be glad not to meet. (Military Scene)

By February 1991 no decision had been made on their future employment. The Georgia National Guard mobilised the 48th Infantry Brigade (Mechanised) which was originally intended to 'roundout' the 24th Division. It had two mechanised infantry battalions with Bradleys, a tank battalion with M1s and an artillery battalion with M109s. The brigade's commanding officer, Col. (P) W. Altoona Holland, is a carpet manufacturing plant manager in civilian life. The 155th Armoured Brigade from Mississippi mustered some 120 M1 tanks and 54 Bradleys. Its 3,900 soldiers were originally intended to 'roundout' the 1st Cavalry Division. The 256th Infantry Brigade (Mechanised) of the Louisiana National Guard was organised in a similar way to the 48th Brigade and fields 65 M1s and 100 Bradleys. Brig.Gen. Garry Whipple had 4,777 men in his brigade.

Further deployments in the second wave virtually doubled the number of Marines in the region to almost 90,000. The II Marine Amphibious Force was mobilised at Camp Lejeune, North Carolina, to command part of the expanded Marine contingent, with its 2nd Marine Division joining the 1st Marine Division ashore in eastern Saudi Arabia. US amphibious capability was enhanced by the deployment of an additional Amphibious Task Group centred on the USS *Tarawa* and the 5th Marine Expeditionary Brigade. In January 1991 this expanded amphibious force carried out manoeuvres on the coast of Oman to build on expertise gained during similar exercises on the Saudi coast in November 1991 code-named Exercise Imminent Thunder. Some 800 USMC reservists were also mobilised by President Bush to support the additional Marine Corps units moving to the Gulf. Units mobilised included tank, infantry, amphibious assault, military police, headquarters, engineer, reconnaissance, anti-aircraft and transport elements.

By late January 1991 US forces in the Middle East numbered some 475,000 men, 260,000 from the US Army, 75,000 sailors, 90,000 US Marines and 50,000 airmen. The final elements of VII Corps were still moving into Saudi Arabia after storms in the Bay of Biscay delayed their shipping. VII Corps units already in the country were carrying out final training before moving forward to their assembly areas near the Iraqi–Saudi border. XVIII Corps units had already moved to this region, with the 1st (British) Armoured Division in support. Helicopters and C-130 transport planes were used to ferry tank crews and infantrymen forward, while huge convoys of tank transporters moved the armour forward. The 1st and 2nd Marine Divisions moved up to near the Kuwait–Saudi border in support of Arab forces already deployed there. Behind the combat units the support commands worked round the clock to stockpile supplies of ammunition and fuel in forward areas using trucks, helicopters and C-130s. To increase the firepower of the two Marine Divisions near Kuwait, the Tiger Brigade of the 2nd Armoured Division, with M1A1 tanks, was detached from VII Corps to support the Marine units in late January.

The Humvee

While hi-tech Patriot surface-to-air missiles or M1A1 tanks may have grabbed all the headlines during the Gulf crisis a more low-tech piece of

A deadly combination – this high mobility Humvee mounts a TOW anti-tank missile launcher capable of knocking out the very best Iraqi armour. Difficult to spot and engage this represents a potent threat to any enemy formation. (Military Scene)

equipment – the HMMWV or Humvee – was ensuring that US troops got into the battle zone or had the right supplies to do their job.

HMMWV is the US military designation for the High Mobility Multi-purpose Wheeled Vehicle, but it soon became known to the troops as the Humvee. It traces its ancestry back to the famous World War Two Willys Jeep and has taken over many of the roles of the classic vehicle. The successor company to Willys Overland, AM General, produced their first HMMWV prototype in 1981 which eventually won a Pentagon competition for a new utility vehicle.

A stiff battle with Congressional budget cutters ensued before the HMMWV was officially accepted into service. AM General, however, did not survive this struggle and it was the victim of a corporate take-over by LTV Aerospace and Defence Company in 1983. Soon the first of 60,000 HMMWVs were flowing off the production line at Mishawaka, Indiana, in 15 different versions for the US Army, Marine Corps and Navy. It replaced the M151 $\frac{1}{4}$-ton truck, M561/M792 Gama Goat and M880 series.

The HMMWV is designed to operate in all types of terrain and climates. It is fully air-portable and air-droppable. A C-130 Hercules can take three of the vehicles, a C-141 Starlifter six, a C-5 Galaxy 15 and the CH-47 Chinook and CH-53 Sea Stallion can both carry two.

In its standard form, the M998, the HMMWV can seat three people, and has a top speed of 105 km/h. It has a range of 482 km on a 94.9-litre fuel tank. The gross weight of the vehicle is 3,465 kg and it can carry a 1,125 kg payload internally or 1,530 kg when towing a trailer. A 6.2-litre V8 diesel engine powers the HMMWV through an automatic three-speed gear box.

The M998 general purpose unarmoured cargo/troop carrier is supplemented by the M1038, which is very similar but equipped with a winch. Three ambulance versions have been built, the M996, M997 and M1035, of which two are armoured. Two shelter-carrying vehicles, the M1037 and M1042, are in service. There are four armed versions, which all have armoured bodies. The M1043 is fitted with a 12.7 mm machine-gun. Other armed versions are the M1025, M1026 and M1044. The standard US Army TOW anti-tank missile armed version is the M1045, which is based on an armoured body. Other TOW versions are the M966, M1036 and M1046. The M1069 is designed as a gun tractor for the M119 105 mm Light Gun and can carry its six-man crew, 22 rounds and gun spares.

US MILITARY DOCTRINE

America's defeat in Vietnam had a profound effect on the US Military and its doctrine. The US Army and Air Force profoundly questioned the way the Vietnam War had been fought and sought to go back to a traditional war-fighting strategy. In particular they rejected the concept of using force for limited political aims and escalating violence to bring the enemy to the conference table. This was seen as forcing the US to fight with one hand behind its back and locking America into a war of attrition.

In the 10 years following the end of the Vietnam War the American Military came round to the view that ground forces should only be committed to achieve decisive military victory. Overwhelming Force would have to be employed to defeat enemies

This Marine takes a drink through his NBC protective hoods. Desert conditions would have made any prolonged use of this gear a sure route to rapid heat exhaustion. (Military Scene)

high technology. The envelopment and subsequent destruction of the enemy's armed forces was to take place in many dimensions, on land, in the air, electronically and psychologically, in all weathers, terrain and climates. This stress on the destruction of enemy armed forces intrinsically rejected the ideas that had governed US strategy in Vietnam. Whereas in Vietnam violence was escalated deliberately in attempts to force political concessions from the enemy, in AirLand Battle all military forces are to be utilised as soon as possible in an unlimited way to militarily defeat the enemy. The territorial limitations on operations that allowed the North Vietnamese sanctuary in Laos and Cambodia and checked any land operations in North Vietnam are also rejected in AirLand Battle. The enemy has to be sought out wherever he is hiding and killed.

AirLand Battle is not a rigid doctrine but a concept of operations that can be used from battalion up to theatre level, anywhere in the world. To enable US Army units to put it into practice a massive re-equipment and training programme was carried out during the 1980s, culminating in the 'Army of Excellence' reorganisations of the late-1980s. Under this programme every manoeuvre unit – battalion, brigade, division or corps – was given the capability to fight in front of, deep behind or above the enemy and to paralyse his command capability.

The division is the basic formation and it is provided with three ground manoeuvre brigades formed with a mix of tanks, mechanised infantry, airborne infantry or airmobile troops, a combat aviation brigade of helicopters, long-range artillery units with remote target acquisition support, highly mobile ground and air reconnaissance assets, electronic warfare units, air defence and integrated supply units. The type of divisional formation may differ depending on its role: either heavy armour or light infantry or airmobile, but the mix of arms to all types of divisions was standard to enable them to apply the 'AirLand Battle' concept. Command systems were highly flexible to allow divisions to be broken down into brigades and battalions but still allow for them to retain the full mix of forces needed to operate 'AirLand Battle' on a smaller scale. Going up the chain of command, corps and armies contained the same mix of forces as divisions but on a large scale.

quickly with minimum loss of US lives. US operations in Grenada and Panama illustrated the use of the Overwhelming Force concept. The messy US retreat from Lebanon further convinced US military leaders of the limited utility of committing US ground forces on dubious political adventures with limited objectives.

This return to a traditional war strategy finally took shape in the 'AirLand Battle' concept of Army Field Manual FM 100-5 in 1982. It envisaged the US Army defeating the enemy by the use of all the latest

UNIT ORGANIZATION

Heavy divisions are termed armoured, mechanised infantry or cavalry divisions, but the names are really only used for administrative or historical reasons. They are all basically the same and they only differ slightly in the mix of tank and mechanised infantry battalions depending on their base location. Divisions based in Germany generally field more battalions and have a higher percentage of tank battalions than continental USA-based units, reflecting the greater Soviet tank threat in Europe. Germany-based divisions also usually field two attack helicopter battalions in their combat aviation brigades rather than one as in US-based divisions.

Germany-based heavy divisions field 10 manoeuvre battalions, usually with six or five of them being tank battalions. Each division has four brigade headquarters, three ground and one aviation, which are assigned forces – tank, infantry or helicopters – depending on the task they are required to perform. Within brigades, battalion headquarters are assigned companies depending on their specific task. They are termed Task Force and take the designation of the unit headquarters commanding the mixed force. For example if the 1st Battalion, 315th Infantry (Mechanised) Regiment was formed into a combined arms force it would adopt the designation Task Force 315. Unlike the British combined arms concept, which allows for company-sized all-arms groups to be formed, the US concept sees the company as the smallest unit to be split up between task forces.

The use of tanks and mechanised infantry to surround and destroy enemy formations dates back to World War II, but in the integration of helicopters into battlefield operations the US Army has transformed its tactical thinking, making AirLand Battle a reality. Each division has attack helicopter battalions which field either 22 AH-1 Cobras or 18 AH-64 Apaches and 13 OH-58 scout helicopters. A company of assault helicopters with around 15 UH-60 Black-

---

Major Central Command US Army Units

XVIII Airborne Corps
  18th Aviation Brigade
  18th Field Artillery Brigade
  12th Aviation Brigade
  III Corps Artillery
  82nd Airborne Division
  101st Airborne Division (Air Assault)
  24th Infantry Division (Mechanised)
  1st Cavalry Division
  3rd Armoured Cavalry Regiment

VII Corps
  11th Aviation Brigade
  17th Field Artillery Brigade
  72nd Field Artillery Brigade
  210th Field Artillery Brigade
  1st Armoured Division
  3rd Armoured Division
  1st Infantry Division (Mechanised)
  2nd Armoured Cavalry Regiment

TOTAL: 2,500 main battle tanks
       1,400 battlefield helicopters

A Combat Engineering Tractor (CET) operating alongside a Fascine carrier. It was engineering vehicles such as these which bridged and punched holes in the Iraqi defensives clearing the way for the coalition spearhead. (Military Scene)

A platoon of four M1s manoeuvre carefully into hull-down positions behind a sandbank. The coordination of movement and firepower is the key to modern armoured warfare. (US DoD via Tim Ripley)

hawks complete the combat aviation brigade. At a corps level combat aviation brigades muster three or four attack battalions, one or two assault companies and a battalion of 24 CH-47 Chinook transport helicopters.

Attack helicopters have both offensive and defensive roles. Their tasks are rapid response to enemy tank breakthroughs, offensive air attacks on frontline enemy positions, deep penetration missions to destroy targets of opportunity ahead of friendly tank columns pushing into enemy territory and flank protection of such formations. The UH-60s and CH-47s also give American commanders the ability to rapidly move troops around the battlefield and carry out 'vertical envelopment' of enemy positions. One US division, the 101st Airborne, is trained and equipped solely for this mission. It has some 350 attack and assault helicopters to enable it to move one complete brigade of three infantry battalions deep behind enemy lines in one lift.

United States Marine Corps

Due to its specialist role as America's amphibious assault corps the US Marines have had an all-arms combat doctrine since World War II. Their island-hopping campaign in the Pacific against the Japanese taught the Marines the need to have all-arms integrated effectively at all levels of command.

During the post-war period this evolved into what is known as the Marine Air-Ground Task Force (MAGTF) concept to enable amphibious assaults to be carried out successfully by units from company to divisional size. In many ways it predated AirLand Battle, particularly in the use of helicopters to support and transport ground troops. Amphibious

US Marine Expeditionary Brigade
Main units:
   2–5 infantry battalions
   tank company
   artillery battalion
   reconnaissance company
   amphibious assault company
   engineer company
   SEAL-special forces team

Total manpower: 15,000

Equipment:
   17 M60 tanks
   24 M109 155 mm self-propelled howitzers
   6 M110 203 mm self-propelled howitzers
   24 115 mm towed howitzers
   24 LAV wheeled armoured vehicles
   47 LVTP amphibious assault vehicles
   48 TOW anti-tank missiles
   72 Dragon anti-tank missiles
   24 81 mm mortars

forces, by their very nature, lack the heavy armour and artillery of conventional ground forces, so the US Marines saw the close integration of air support as an effective way of compensating for their lack of tanks and artillery.

MAGTF is mission-orientated, so Marine combat formations are formed to carry out particular tasks. There are three main types of MAGTF. The largest type is the Marine Amphibious Force (MAF), which fields a full division of all-arms ground troops and an air wing of more than 20 squadrons of AV-8B Harriers and F-18 strike aircraft, CH-53 and CH-47 transport helicopters and AH-1 Cobra attack helicopters. All the Marine aircraft are able to operate from US Navy carriers or rough forward airstrips. The introduction of the V/STOL AV-8Bs has even made it possible for them to operate alongside helicopters on amphibious assault ships. Marine Expeditionary Brigades (MEB) contain a regimental-sized ground force and a mixed air group of some half a dozen squadrons. The smallest-sized unit is the Marine Amphibious Unit (MAU), which is based around a ground battalion and is supported by a composite air squadron.

During the 1970s there was much debate about the future of the US Marine Corps with some sections of the Pentagon pressing for it to move more towards mechanised units tailored to fight in a European conflict against Soviet tank formations. This move was resisted by the Marines and they took up the Rapid Deployment Joint Task Force (RDJTF) concept with enthusiasm. Third World intervention operations became their main *raison d'être*. Large sums of money were devoted to purchasing equipment to preposition on ships in the Indian Ocean for use in emergencies. The US Marines 'lean and mean' equipment policy continued to prevent their mobility being hampered by large amounts of heavy tanks and other armoured vehicles. This enabled quick responses by the US Marines during the Grenada conflict, the Lebanon intervention and in the first weeks of Operation Desert Shield.

THE BRITISH ARMY DEPLOYS

British reaction to the Iraqi invasion of Kuwait was swift, and within days of the crisis breaking, ships and aircraft had been ordered to the Middle East to help protect Saudi Arabia and other Gulf states.

The involvement of British Army troops was at first limited to assisting the RAF and providing military assistance to Gulf allies armed forces. Operation Granby 1, as the first British deployment operation commitment was code-named, got under way on 9 August when RAF Tornado F3 fighters touched down at Dhahran in eastern Saudi Arabia to help the Allied air defence screen.

Detachments of 30 Signals Regiment, from Blandford, deployed detachments equipped with the new vehicle satellite communications equipment (VCS 501) to provide communications links for RAF units based at Dhahran and Riyadh in Saudi Arabia, Thumrait and Seeb in Oman, and with the RAF on Bahrain. The detachment at Thumrait had to work in primitive conditions and 54-degree temperatures. When the RAF Jaguars at Thumrait redeployed to Bahrain the Royal Signals detachment packed up shop and moved to support 7th Armoured Brigade in eastern Saudi Arabia. As RAF deployments to Saudi Arabia continued, a further detachment took up residence at Tabuk airbase in western Saudi Arabia to support RAF Tornado GR1s based there.

To provide medical support for the RAF, Royal Navy and Army units moving into the Gulf region, 22

If fuel is the lifeblood of armoured formations then water is of equal importance to any desert operation and DROPS vehicles such as this one ensured supplies of this vital commodity. (MoD Army public relations)

This 7th Brigade corporal on 'stag' at dusk defends his heavily sandbagged position with what appears to be a modified Bren gun, still an effective and reliable weapon. (Military Scene)

Field Hospital established itself near the RAF base on Bahrain. A 29-strong surgical team from the unit was already in Dhahran to support the RAF.

Elements of 22nd Special Air Service Regiment and the Special Boat Squadron were flown out to Saudi Arabia late in August, reportedly equipped with large quantities of laser target markers to help RAF Jaguars deliver smart bombs on to their targets.

The armed forces of most of Britain's Gulf allies were without any defence against Iraqi chemical weapons so a major effort was mounted to provide them with Nuclear, Biological and Chemical (NBC) warfare protective equipment and advice. Teams of instructors from the NBC Centre at Winterbourne Gunner, assisted by British Aerospace personnel and members of the Territorial Army, were quickly despatched to Saudi Arabia and other Gulf states. The instructors worked at locations all over Saudi Arabia to enable local forces to withstand an Iraqi chemical attack. Part of their task was also to collect samples of any Iraqi chemical agents used against coalition forces and quickly return them to the Chemical Warfare Establishment at Porton Down for analysis.

The Desert Rats

Although Britain's rapid reaction force, the 5th Airborne Brigade, was alerted soon after the invasion of Kuwait they were never deployed when it became clear that heavy armoured units would be needed to counter Iraq's 5,500 tanks.

On 14 September 1990 British Defence Secretary Tom King announced that the 7th Armoured Brigade, commanded by Brig. Patrick Cordingley, would be moved from its base at Fallingbostel in Germany to Saudi Arabia to support the US Marine Corps' I Marine Amphibious Force. The Brigade's deployment immediately evoked memories of the World War II campaign in North Africa, but serious military reasons, rather than sentimentality, lay behind the choice of the unit to spearhead Britain's Middle East commitment. It possessed the Army's modern Challenger tanks and the new Warrior infantry fighting vehicle. Its armoured infantry battalion, 1st Battalion The Staffordshire Regiment, had also recently returned from intense training on the giant Suffield training area in Canada.

In theory the brigade was a well-equipped and powerful formation, but it was far from ready to be shipped out to Saudi Arabia. Many regiments in the British Army of the Rhine (BAOR) were under-manned because of recruiting problems, the need to supply manpower for Northern Ireland and other tasks. A fire at the main tank spare parts warehouse at Donnington had also reduced the flow of parts to units in Germany to a trickle, putting many vehicles off the road.

A crash programme was put in train to bring the brigade up to strength, repaint vehicles in desert camouflage and carry out last-minute gunnery and NBC training. The Scots Dragoon Guards swapped their Challenger Mk 1s for the more modern Mk 3 versions belonging to the Life Guards and also stripped their Mk 1s of any useful spares. Complete troops of tank crews from the 14th/20th King's Hussars and 17th/21st Lancers were also drafted in to make up numbers. The brigade's other armoured regiment, The Queen's Royal Irish Hussars, was reinforced by four troops from the 17th/21st Lancers which were attached to each of its squadrons. The Staffords were reinforced by a company of the Grenadier Guards, while 40 Field Regiment received elements of 43 and 21 Air Defence Batteries equipped with the hand-held Javelin surface-to-air missile.

Eventually the Desert Rats, as the 7th Brigade were now universally known, were ready to go and their vehicles were despatched to Bremerhaven docks for shipment to Saudi Arabia in late September and early October. While the vehicles and equipment were afloat, the troops carried out more training before flying out to Saudi Arabia on RAF and chartered transport aircraft.

As the combat units of 7th Armoured Brigade were making their preparations to move from their German bases, a major operation was in progress to ensure their arrival in Saudi Arabia went smoothly. The first task to be undertaken was the construction of a massive tent city at the Saudi port of Jubayl to accommodate the brigade while it collected its equipment after unloading from the chartered transport ships and Royal Fleet Auxilliary landing ships. Known officially as the Force Maintenance Area (FMA) but dubbed Balbrick Lines by its residents, the tent city was constructed from scratch by Royal Engineers of 39 Engineer Regiment, who were flown out from the UK at short notice to start their Herculean task.

Medical support was boosted by the arrival of 33 Field Hospital and 15 RAF Puma helicopters supported by medics of 24 (Airmobile) Field Ambulance. A number of regimental bands, including those of the King's Own Border regiment, 13th/18th Hussars, Hampshire Regiment, Green Howards, Light Infantry, Devon and Dorset Regiment and Parachute Regiment, were also flown out to provide additional medical support and man NBC decontamination facilities.

A major logistic supply system was set up to support the 7th Brigade with large ammunition, water pillow tanks and fuel dumps being established deep in the desert in preparation for operations against the Iraqis. The supply dump system stretched from Jubayl out to the 7th Brigade's deployment area. 10 Regiment, Royal Corps of Transport, had 80 14-ton Foden lorries and 60 of the new DROPS vehicles, which were being used in large numbers for the first time for the bulk distribution of water. DROPS – Demountable Rack Off-Loading and Pick-Up System – was put into service by the regiment a month early for Operation Granby. It enables containers to be put on and off trucks by an integrally mounted hydraulic lifting device. This speeds up loading and cuts out the need for fork-lift trucks. The regiment's tank transporter troop played a key role moving armour from the docks out into the desert to save wear and tear on tracked vehicles. New roads were also built into the desert by 21 Engineer Regiment's three field squadrons.

Elements of 17 Port Regiment, Royal Corps of Transport, were on hand to unload the ships carrying the 7th Brigade's vehicles when they arrived at Jubayl. Before the ships came into dock, Royal Navy minesweepers cleared a channel to ensure that no Iraqi mines interrupted the unloading.

To prepare the 7th Brigade for combat a series of live firing exercises was conducted on improvised firing ranges out in the desert. A team of experts from the Royal Artillery Gunnery School at Larkhill, the

British Infantry storm a trench system during a live fire exercise. The lead figure carries a PRC-349 radio, used by section commanders and second-in-command. (MoD Army public relations)

Before the advent of the Warrior the FV432 was the standard British APC. This 7th Brigade specimen carries a cheerful looking group of passengers and a rather sullen looking American colleague. (Military Scene)

Royal Armoured Corps Gunnery School at Larkhill, the Gunnery Wing at Hohne in Germany and the Small Arms School Corps flew out to construct the range, which was predictably soon nicknamed Jerboa Range. Each battlegroup of the 7th Brigade took turns to go down the eight-mile-long live firing 'battle run' to fine tune their all-arms combat skills. The range was patrolled every morning, ensuring wandering Bedouin tribesmen didn't stray into the danger zone. All weapons in the brigade were fired on the range, from infantrymen's SA-80s to M109 155mm howitzers of 40 Field regiment and Giant Viper mine-clearing devices of 25 Engineer Regiment, Royal Engineers.

At this phase of the Gulf crisis the American and British forces were deployed in defensive positions behind the Arab forces positioned along the Kuwait border. The 7th Brigade was integrated with the US Marines positioned around Jubayl. A detachment of Royal Signals was established at the 1st US Marine Division's headquarters to co-ordinate their operations, USMC HAWK surface-to-air missile batteries provided air defence for British units and USMC forward air controllers were attached to the 7th Brigade. They were of great importance because the 7th Brigade relied on the USMC for air support and helicopter transport. It had been decided not to send any British helicopters to Saudi Arabia at this stage of Operation Granby due to logistic problems of

using helicopters in the desert. The integration of the British brigade to the USMC was a logical move given the lack of armour available to the US Marines.

1st (British) Armoured Division

After the US decision in early November 1990 to almost double its Operation Desert Shield commitment by despatching another 200,000 troops to Saudi Arabia, Defence Secretary Tom King announced on 22 November the Britain would also be significantly boosting the offensive capability of its forces in the Middle East.

The expanded British Force contained some of the British Army's most powerful artillery and combat engineer units to enable it to break through the massive Iraqi defences around Kuwait. Its main combat formation was the 4th Armoured Brigade, with a tank regiment, two armoured infantry battalions, artillery and supporting arms. An air defence and two heavy artillery regiments formed the Divisional Artillery Group.

Under the command of Maj.Gen. Rupert Smith, the 1st Division moved out to Saudi Arabia just before Christmas 1990 and took over command of the 7th Brigade. In the first weeks of its deployment the division remained close to the US Marines around Jubayl, but as the UN deadline loomed in January 1991 it started to move further inland, giving the British the option of supporting the US marines or he heavy US tank formations gathering on the Saudi–Iraqi border.

The preparations to get 1st Division out to the desert followed the pattern successfully established by the 7th Brigade. Operation Granby 1.5 began with intense work taking place in Germany to bring units up to strength, prepare vehicles, load equipment for shipment out to the Gulf and carry out final refresher training. Again many men had to be drafted in to bring units up to their wartime strength; sometimes it involved individual soldiers or whole units being cross-posted. The 1st Battalion The Scots Guards had the Queen's Company, 1st Battalion The Grenadier Guards attached for Operation Granby 1.5. 2 Field Regiment was reinforced by the Javelin-armed 46 Air Defence Battery. Feverish work took place at German garrisons supplying units to the division. One unfortunate officer from the Queen's Own Highlanders fell victim to the mad rush to paint every piece of equipment sand pink and one morning found his VW Beetle had a new coat of desert camouflage.

Massive fire support for the 1st Division was provided by 39 Heavy Regiment with 12 of the new Multiple Launch Rocket System (MLRS). It was nicknamed the 'battlewinner' or 'grid square removal service' because of its multiple warhead system, which distributed 644 M77 bomblets over a large area at ranges up to 25 miles. Conventional heavy tube artillery was provided by 32 Heavy Regiment, which mustered 12 203 mm M110 self-propelled howitzers and 16 155 mm M109 self-propelled howitzers. Divisional air defence was provided by the Rapier surface-to-air missile launchers of 12 Air Defence

Regiment. 32 Armoured Engineer Regiment equipped with large numbers of armoured engineering vehicles provided the division with a capability to breach Iraqi field defences. The regiment's Chieftain armoured bridges, Giant Viper mine-clearing rockets, FV180 Combat Engineering Tractors (CET) and Centurion AVREs are all designed to enable engineers to blast holes through minefields and field defences for follow-on forces to pass through and engage the enemy. These units are normally considered as 'corps assets' and their deployment with 1st Division indicated the offensive nature of the increased British contribution to the coalition ground forces.

When planning 1st Division's deployment it was decided to give the formation its own integrated national helicopter support, unlike 7th Brigade which had to rely on the US marines' large aviation assets. 4 Army Air Corps Regiment supplied 23 Gazelle AH.1 observation helicopters and 23 Lynx AH.7 TOW-armed anti-tank helicopters. Its three squadrons, 654, 659 and 661, provided 1st Division with a fast-moving airborne anti-tank and reconnaissance force. For transport and casualty evaluation the Support Helicopter Force (SHF) was formed from Royal Air Force and Fleet Air Arm assets. Its first helicopters, 15 RAF Puma HC1s and 3 Chinook HC1s, were flown out to Saudi Arabia by USAF C-5 Galaxy aircraft in November 1990 and it was brought up to full strength in January 1991, when the chartered cargo ship *Atlantic Conveyor* arrived in Saudi waters. On board the ship were vehicles of the Commando Helicopter Operations and Support Cell, eight RAF Chinook HC1s of Nos. 7 and 18 Squadrons and

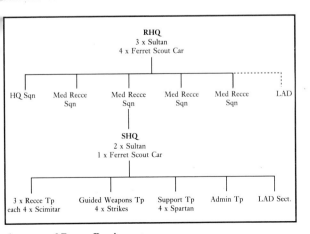

Armoured Recce Regiment

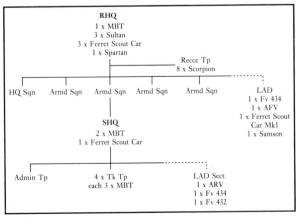

Armoured Regiment

THE PLATES

A: An M60A3 fitted with a mine plough and 'Blazer' reactive armour plates. The reactive armour is mounted on a metal frame on the turret and explodes when struck by an incoming round or rocket directing the force of the explosion away from the vehicle and thus greatly reducing the penetration of the enemy round. The mine plough on this vehicle and the dozer blade on that next to it show how seriously coalition forces treated the threat from Iraqi mines. Visible on the 'Blazer' plates on the forward part of the turret are the inverted chevron invasion markings adopted by the coalition and added just days before the land battle. (Military Scene)

B: A Spartan MCT equipped with a Euromissile MILAN compact turret over the roof, with two missiles in the ready to launch position. MILAN can engage enemy vehicles out to a range of 2000 m, and makes the Spartan MCT a very potent weapon. In addition to the two missiles in the launcher, 11 are carried internally, seven on the left side and four on the right. The Commander's hatch is open obscuring the 7.62 mm machine gun mounted on the right hand side of the No16 cupola which can be aimed and fired from inside the vehicle. The red jerboa of 7th Brigade is visible in front of the storage racks on the vehicle's side. (Military Scene)

C: Lt. Gen. Sir Peter de la Billiere is the first general to wear his general officers' cap badge in the sand coloured beret of the SAS. He served with 22nd SAS Regt and SAS Group for many years, and of his 38 years' service a total of 20 have been spent in the Middle East. It is thus hardly surprising that he speaks Arabic fluently. His slip-on rank insignia are the crossed sword and baton with crown of a Lieutenant General. (Military Scene)

D1: This dugout is just one of those manned by US Army personnel defending the approaches to Dhahran Airbase in Saudi Arabia. This emplacement has been heavily sandbagged against enemy attack but the only weapon visible is what appears to be an M-16 slung over the right shoulder of the figure on the left and neither man wears desert pattern camouflage. With US forces making up the largest contingent of the coalition forces in the Gulf theatre it was natural that they should bear a proportionally larger burden in providing rear area security, and the defence of many key installations fell to US personnel. (US DoD via Robert F. Dorr)

D2: This M2 Bradley on the dockside in Saudi Arabia is obviously a recent arrival as the tape applied before shipping has not been removed from the gun barrel, the TOW launcher or the sight. This vehicle has not yet been resprayed for desert operations and remains in its European Theatre camouflage. In addition to the McDonnell Douglas Helicopter Company M242 25 mm Chain Gun and M240C 7.62 mm coax machine gun, the Bradley carries a Hughes Aircraft Corporation two-tube TOW launcher which enables it to engage enemy armour out to a maximum range of 3750 m. The launcher is shown here retracted and lying along the left side of the turret for travelling. (Military Scene)

E: A Ferret Mk2 Scout Car armed with a turret mounted 7.62 mm Browning machine gun. The Ferret is used as a liaison vehicle in Armoured, Recce and Engineer units, and the Commander of this one has provided himself with a little extra insurance in the form of the SLR hanging on the right side of the turret. Note the smoke discharges on the forward hull; those on the right hand side of the vehicle are partly obscured by the headlight. The metal plate hanging on the front of the Scout Car has been acquired to help get the vehicle out of soft sand. (MoD Army Public Relations)

F: Infantry of the 1st Staffordshires take a break to write 'blueys' home. The red jerboa badge of the 7th Brigade is clearly visible on the right sleeve of the figure seated left-centre. There is a mixture of 'rust and sand' desert combat suits and European pattern DPM; several wear lightweight Combat Body Armour in new desert camouflage and their SA.80 Individual Weapons have been hastily camouflaged with sand paint which is already showing signs of wear and tear. Even their packs have been daubed with sand paint in an effort to break up their outline. (MoD Army Public Relations)

G1: A Challenger crew busy themselves with routine maintenance and the camouflaging of their position. The name 'Antrim' on the side of the vehicle suggests that this is probably the Queens Royal Irish Hussars. The thermal sleeve and muzzle reference system are clearly visible on the barrel of the 120 mm L11A5 rifled tank gun. The box on the right side of the turret is the armoured container for the Thermal Imaging Surveillance and Gun Sighting Sights, also known as TOGS (Thermal Observation and Gunnery Sights). (MoD Army Public Relations)

G2: Some of the best of the Arab coalition troops, the Syrian soldiers sent to the Gulf were largely veteran troops with combat experience in Lebanon. This unit, parading for inspection by King Fahd of Saudi Arabia, are particularly well turned out with modern pattern helmets (with one exception), webbing including ammunition pouches for their Soviet AKMS assault rifles and uncharacteristically clean camouflaged battle dress. They are all also equipped with Soviet pattern gas masks hanging on their left hip. (Military Scene)

H: A Reconnaisance Troop Scorpion of one of 7th Brigades Armoured Regiments. Powered by the Jaguar J60 No1 Mk 100B 4.2 litre, 6 cylinder engine, the scorpion has the very respectable top road speed of 80 km/h. The soft sand of the desert reduces this capability but armed with its 76 mm L23 gun it remains a potent recce asset. The main armament is a lighter version of the L5 used in the Saladin armoured car and fires Canister, HESH (High Explosive Squash Head), HE, Smoke and illumination. A four-barrelled, electrically operated smoke discharger is usually fitted to the vehicle, but in this case only a three-barrelled version is carried. The Scorpion is also fitted with a coax 7.62 mm machine gun mounted to the left of the main armament which can be used as a ranging machine gun. (MoD Army Public Relations)

I: The M551A Sheridans of the 82nd Airborne Division were the first American armoured vehicles to arrive in Saudi Arabia. The unusual 152 mm calibre of the main armament is the result of its

An M60A3 with reactive armour and mine plough

A

B

Lt. Gen. Sir Peter de la Billiere

1

US Army dugout defending Dhahran

2

D   An M2 Bradley on the dockside in Saudi Arabia

A Ferret Mk2 Scout Car

F Infantry of the 1st Staffordshires

A Challenger under camouflage nets

Syrian troops parade for King Fahd of Saudi Arabia

H

An M551A Sheridan of the 82nd Airborne Division

I

1

A sandbagged machine gun nest

2

Brig. Hammerbeck's Land Rover 110

Corporal, USMC, Saudi desert

K

L

Two Challengers replenishing ammunition

N   Military Police corporal, 4th Brigade

MCV80 Warrior, Saudi desert

Chieftain ARRV with Challenger powerpack

P

being designed as a dual purpose gun/launcher for the MGM-57 Shillelagh anti-tank guided missile which is no longer in service. The extensive armour plating around the commander's .50 calibre machine gun was a modification added after the Vietnam War where commanders operating the machine gun proved dangerously exposed to enemy small arms fire. (US DoD via Tim Ripley)

J1: This sandbagged machine gun nest is part of the defences of one of the central supply depots in the rear. The L7A1 GPMG has now largely been replaced in frontline British service by the SA.80 SAW but is retained for rear echelon units and still provides the standard vehicle-mounted machine gun in the British Army. The belt-fed ammunition is alternating tracer and ball; the high proportion of tracer ammunition allows greater accuracy, particularly in night engagements. (MoD Army Public Relations)

J2: Three SLR armed members of the 4th Armoured Brigade keep a watchful eye on Brigadier Christopher Hammerbeck's Land Rover 110. They have traded in the helmets for desert pattern bush hats and have also received their desert boots which were produced in record time for issue to the troops in the Gulf. Of the units comprising 4th Brigade, only 14th/20th King's Hussars is an element of the original BAOR 4th Brigade; the two mechanized infantry battalions (1st Bn. The Royal Scots (The Royal Regiment), 3rd Bn. The Royal Regiment of Fusiliers) appear to have been drawn from 6th Armoured Brigade. (Military Scene)

K: This US Marine Corps Corporal wears Desert Battle Dress Uniform (BDU) with a similar pattern camouflage cover for his 'Fritz' Kevlar PASGT (Personnel Armour system for Ground Troops) helmet. His webbing is worn over a PASGT flak jacket which is in temperate climate camouflage pattern. The sunglasses are not simply a fashion statement but represent a very effective way of reducing glare and improving vision in the desert environment. The M203 which he carries is a development of a Vietnam-era weapon and combines a 40 mm grenade launcher with the M-16 rifle. (Military Scene)

L: The crew of this Warrior are fitting storage racks to add to its already considerable storage capacity. The MCV80 carries eight infantrymen (one of whom also commands the vehicle and therefore dismounts with the infantry) and a gunner and driver. It also carries all the equipment required to fight on the battlefield for a period of 48 hours. The two-man steel turret is in the centre of the vehicle offset slightly to the left of the vehicle's centre line and has power traverse with manual controls for emergency use. The commander and gunner have a Pilkington PE Raven day/night sight, the commander's having additional traverse, with periscopes giving vision to the sides and rear of the turret. The temperate climate pattern DPM suggests that these are rear echelon troops. (MoD Army Public Relations)

M: Two Challengers replenishing their ammunition after expending a considerable amount of their on-board supply. Note the charge bags on top of the turret of the lead Challenger. Unlike the Americans, the British use two-piece ammunition of charge and projectile which allows a larger number of projectiles to be carried. There are up to 42 charge stowage positions and 64 projectile; a usual mix is 20 DS (Discarding Sabot) and 44 HESH/Smoke. All charges are stowed in special containers with fire suppressant fluid below the turret ring reducing the risk of ammunition fires. It is likely that this scene is early in the conflict as the crews have not been issued with the desert boots developed for use in the Gulf. (MoD Army Public Relations)

N: This corporal of 4th Brigade's Military Police wears European pattern DPM battle dress which appears to have been relatively common for personnel operating in rear areas. Over this he had added desert pattern lightweight Combat Body Armour. His DPM brassard carries 'MP' in black on a red panel below the miniature subdued badge of rank. Above both of these he wears the current 4th Armoured Brigade patch; this is a revival of the wartime shape with a black jerboa on pale brown khaki. He is also equipped with what appears to be L2A3 Stirling submachine gun. (Military Scene)

O1: This warrior is festooned with extra containers and equipment, which, although making it look rather cluttered, perform a far more practical purpose. The bundle of bergens and packs secured to the front of the vehicle help protect it from enemy fire, particularly Rocket Propelled Grenades (RPG), with which the Iraqis were liberally equipped. This view also shows clearly the positioning of the Perkins Engines Condor CV8 TCA diesel engine to the right of the driver (whose hatch is open); developing some 550 hp this engine gives the Warrior a top road speed of around 75 km/h making it one of the world's fastest APCs. (MoD Army Public Relations)

O2: A Chieftain ARRV (Armoured Repair and Recovery Vehicle) helping to replace the powerpack of a Challenger, which weighs in at 5.49 tonnes. The Challenger is powered by a Perkins Engines (Shrewsbury), Condor 12V 1200 diesel engine which is fitted with two turbo-chargers. The powerpack has been specifically designed for quick replacement in the field and can be removed by a REME (Royal Electrical and Mechanical Engineers) Light Aid Detachment in under 45 minutes. The 1200 bhp developed by the engine gives the Challenger the very respectable top speed of 54 km/h. (MoD Army Public Relations)

P: Adopted as the replacement for the FV432 series of vehicles, the MCV80 Warrior has proved to be an unqualified success. Designed by GKN Sankey, the Warrior beat off competition from the American Bradley to provide the British Army with its Armoured Personnel Carrier for the 1990's. This vehicle has been extensively up-armoured with additional plates added along the side skirts, and camouflage netting has been added to break up the outline of the turret; it cannot disguise the formidable profile of the RARDEN 30 mm cannon. Mounted coaxially with the cannon is a 7.62 mm EX-34 Chain Gun (British designation L94A1). The combination provided the British infantrymen with a firepower and mobility which totally outclassed anything their Iraqi opponents could field against them. (Military Scene)

No. 240 OCU, four RAF Puma HC1s and 12 Sea King HC4 'jungles' of Nos. 845 and 848 Naval Air Squadrons. All the helicopters were fitted with equipment to protect them from desert sand and the Chinooks also boasted newly fitted infra-red jammers, chaff/flare dispensers and two 7.62 mm miniguns.

To support this enlarged British force considerable additional logistic and medical support was provided. One RAF and four Army field hospitals were despatched after the mobilisation of the Territorial Army's 205 General Hospital in December 1991. Every type of support unit needed to keep the fighting troops operational was sent out to the desert from Royal Military Police traffic controllers to extra trucks, cooks, signals units, tank transporters, postal and courier detachments, ordnance experts, tank repair workshops and even a bomb disposal squadron. To extend the 1st Division's logistic chain out into the desert to support its move inland a Forward Force Maintenance Area (FFMA) was established. It was connected to Jubayl by a Military Supply Route (MSR) run by the Royal Military Police. Along the MSR were harbour areas to allow drivers to rest. Four Royal Corps of Transport regiments moved supplies forward to the FFMA, which was protected by giant sand works, or berms, built by the Royal Engineers.

One of the more unusual tasks undertaken was the setting up of a network of navigation beacons in the desert by 14 Independent Topographic Squadron, Royal Engineers. Using the Magellan satellite navigation system they positioned a large number of oil drums mounted in concrete at regular intervals throughout the desert. The drums had geographic co-ordinates painted on the side to help 'lost' Desert Rats confirm their position. This was of particular use to the Royal Artillery, who needed exact navigation equipment to help lay their guns accurately. Thousands of maps were run off the squadron's mobile printing press and its terrain analysis computers provided invaluable information on desert 'going'. To provide increased armour protection for the division's Challengers and Warriors, they were up-armoured at Royal Mechanical Electronic Engineers forward workshops in Saudi Arabia under the supervision of engineers from Vickers and GKN.

The 1st Division's soldiers were made aware that their deployment to Saudi Arabia was a real operational one rather than an extended training exercise by the inclusion of some unusual logistic arrangements. Some 2,000 tank crewmen, infantrymen and gunners were sent out to Saudi Arabia as 'battle casualty replacements' along with dozens of spare Challenger tanks and other armoured vehicles. They were held at various desert supply bases in readiness to be sent forward to take the place of other soldiers and vehicles put out of action in battle. Three

Although a product of the '70s rather than the '90s the FV103 Spartan still performs vital rôles for the Army including carrying Royal Artillery Javelin manportable SAM teams and providing the transport for Royal Engineer assault teams.

A Scammell Commander, the British Army's purpose built Tank transporter. The figure standing just forward of the double wheel-arch illustrates the massive dimensions of this monstrous vehicle. (MoD Army Public Relations)

infantry battalions, 1st Battalion The Grenadier Guards, 1st Battalion King's Own Scottish Borderers and 1st Battalion Royal Highland Fusiliers, were flown out to Saudi Arabia from the UK to provide a guard force for prisoners of war handling facilities being set up by 1st Division.

All the units of the 1st Division had arrived in Saudi Arabia by the time the United Nations deadline for Iraq to withdraw from Kuwait ran out on 16 January 1991. During the first weeks of January, 4th Brigade and other newly arrived combat units carried out field firing to fine tune their weapons and training before deploying deep into the Saudi desert alongside the 7th Brigade. Helicopters of the SHF and RAF C-130 transport planes flew the tank crews, armoured infantrymen and gunners forward to the assembly areas, while more than 100 Scammell Commander tank transporters of 7 Tank Transporter Regiment, Royal Corps of Transport, carried the armoured vehicles.

On 31 January everything was ready and the 1st (British) Armoured Division was declared operational. It only awaited the final confirmatory orders before being launched into battle.

Desert Rat Insignia

When the British 7th Armoured Brigade was ordered to Saudi Arabia in September 1990 it quickly re-adopted the Jerboa or Desert Rat symbol of the old World War II 7th Armoured Division. The rat was adopted by the division during its service in North Africa, where it fought against the German Africa Corps.

After the brigade's vehicles received their sand pink desert camouflage they received a red Desert Rat badge based on a template produced by 14 Topographic Squadron, Royal Engineers. According to tradition the rat should face right, but in the haste to get vehicles painted and out to the Middle East some combat painters had their rats facing left.

All ranks in the brigade also took to wearing a red Desert Rat badge on their right upper sleeve. The badge had a dark blue background.

Not wishing to be outdone, the 4th Armoured Brigade also adopted a type of Desert Rat badge. Its rat was black and the tail was curled above the rat's head. A new brigade motto – 'Hell for leather' – was also adopted by the brigade commander, Brig. Christopher Hammerbeck.

British vehicles were all painted with inverted V air recognition markings to try to enable coalition pilots to avoid mistaking them for Iraqi vehicles. Large orange plastic sheet panels were carried on upper decks of vehicles for the same purpose.

BRITISH ARMOURED WARFARE

In the decade preceding the Gulf crisis the British Army's armoured doctrine had been transformed thanks to new equipment and operational thinking. During the Cold War Britain's armoured forces were concentrated in northern West Germany to counter a

Soviet armoured thrust towards the Rhine and their operational doctrine, tactics and equipment were tailored to meet this threat.

The amount of resources allocated to BAOR and its concept of operations were not always as they should have been. During the 1980s this changed because of increased defence spending by the Conservative government of Margaret Thatcher and new NATO strategies to counter deep Soviet armoured penetrations. During the 1960s and 1970s, BAOR,

---

1st (British) Armoured Division

Division Troops
    16th/5th The Queen's Royal Lancers (recce)
    4 Regiment, Army Air Corps

Divisional Artillery Group
    12 Air Defence Regiment (6 Tracked Rapier SAM, 6 towed Rapier SAM)
    39 Heavy Regiment (12 MLRS)
    32 Heavy Regiment (12 M110 203 mm SP how.)
    26 Field Regiment (16 M109 155 mm SP how.)

4th Armoured Brigade
    14th/20th King's Hussars (57 Challenger MBTs)
    1st Battalion, Royal Scots (45 Warrior APCs)
    3rd Battalion, Royal Regiment of Fusiliers (45 Warrior APCs)
    2 Field Regiment (24 M109 155 mm SP how.)

7th Armoured Brigade
    Queen's Royal Irish Hussars (57 Challenger MBTs)
    Scots Dragoon Guards (57 Challenger MBTs)
    1st Battalion, Staffordshire Regiment (45 Warrior APCs)
    40 Field Regiment (24 M109 155 mm SP how.)
    A Sqn, Queen's Dragoon Guards (12 Scimitar, 4 Striker, 4 Spartan)

Note: During operations companies, squadrons, platoons and troops would be split up between battlegroups and squadron/company groups.

---

while possessing armoured units of great tactical mobility, was strategically a force able only to fight a fixed battle. It had limited logistic support, few helicopters to move air mobile anti-tank teams to block tank breakthroughs, no self-propelled anti-aircraft missiles, outdated armoured personnel carriers and primitive command and control systems. This command weakness would have meant that even if a rapid tank operation needed to be mounted some pundits doubted whether 1st British Corps headquarters would have been able to communicate the orders to subordinate units in time for them to be of any relevance on a fast-moving battlefield.

Under far-sighted commanders such as Generals Sir Nigel Bagnall and Sir Martin Farndale, BAOR was reorganised to enable it to mount rapid counter-strokes against Soviet tank breakthroughs. This was a return to true armoured warfare based on manoeuvre rather than a static war of attrition envisaged under old NATO 'Forward Defence' concepts. BAOR divisions and brigades were trained to carry out operations at fast tempos over long distances and new equipment was introduced to make this new thinking a reality.

New Challenger battle tanks started to replace the Army's worn-out 1960s vintage Chieftains; tracked Rapier was deployed to give the Army mobile air defence; Warrior fighting vehicles gave BAOR's infantry a carrier to match the Soviet BMP and American Bradley; Lynx anti-tank helicopters appeared in large numbers; DROPs supply vehicles transformed BAOR's logistic support; the MLRS rocket system gave BAOR a true deep strike capability and infantrymen received new helmets, NBC kit and the SA-80 small arms system. British tanks also started to be fitted with extra fuel tanks on the rear decking to enable them to operate over long distances. On the communications front, the WAVELL data link system enabled commanders to be provided with realtime computer communications and PTARMIGAN enabled senior commanders to communicate by FAX or telephone in a totally secure way. With almost instantaneous communications British armoured units had their 'flash to bang time' dramatically improved.

All this new kit, as well as boosting morale, made divisional and brigade commanders think in a different way about how to fight an armoured battle. They

This MCV80 Warrior has been extensively up-armoured with additional plates bolted on down the vehicle's side and sports the inverted chevron invasion markings on its turret. (Military Scene)

became more quick thinking and flexible, taking their inspiration more from the German panzer generals such as Erwin Rommel or Heinz Guderian rather than Field Marshal Montgomery. A series of NATO exercises in the early and mid-1980s put flesh on the bones of these new concepts, culminating in Exercise 'Iron Hammer' in November 1989, were a full divisional counter attack was practised against a strong armoured opposing force.

At battalion and company level British armoured warfare doctrine also owes a lot to German World War II experience. During the early years of the North African campaign, British tank and infantry units found themselves outclassed by Rommel's panzer divisions on many occasions because the Germans were better able to operate in all-arms formations known as *Kampfgruppen* or battlegroups. Often British tanks were defeated because they lacked infantry to deal with concealed anti-tank guns or British lorryborne infantry fell victim to surprise panzer attacks. When British armoured formations were reorganised after the war, the German *Kampfgruppe* concept was adopted as the model for brigades, battalion and company level operations.

While in peacetime the infantry battalion or tank regiment was the normal administrative unit and personnel management organisation, during field training the battlegroup became the standard formation. Each infantry battalion headquarters or tank regiment headquarters would be equipped and trained to command mixed formations of tanks, infantry, artillery and engineers. On operations or exercises unit identities broke down and the famous British regimental system ceased to exist. Regimental names are only used to identify battlegroups, i.e., if the Scots Dragoon Guards regimental headquarters were the command element of a mixed infantry battlegroup then it would be known as the 'Scots Dragoon Guards Battlegroup'. The composition of battlegroups is flexible depending on the task it is given; for example, an infantry battalion might exchange one of its companies for a squadron of tanks if it needed an armoured counter attack force to protect its defensive position, while a tank regiment would be given a company of armoured infantry, an artillery battery and an armoured engineering troop if it needed to capture an enemy-occupied hill or village. The lieutenant-colonels in command of British infantry battalions or tank regiments and their staff officers were trained to co-ordinate all-arms formations rather than just their own arm.

The battlegroup may have been the main level of all-arms integration in the British Army, but all-arms concepts are not restricted to this level of command. Moving down the chain of command there are what are known as squadron or company groups, mixing infantry platoons and tank troops. Brigades are also all-arms formations and are allocated battlegroup-sized units by divisional headquarters depending on their objectives and tasking. At all levels of command from company/squadron group up to brigade, there are standard communications equipment, staff and command procedures, to ensure that the Army's all-arms battle concepts are put into practice effectively.

Combat arm tactics are the cutting edge of the British Army, but to keep it fighting a huge logistic tail is necessary. Known as the 'loggies', the Army's logistic support is comprised of units such as the Royal Corps of Transport, Royal Army Ordnance Corps and Royal Mechanical and Electrical Engineers. A dual system of logistic headquarters exists side-by-side with the fighting headquarters, at every level of command. The REME for example has a light aid detachment attached to each battlegroup which is responsible for running repairs on all the vehicles, while at brigade level an armoured workshop is responsible for more serious repairs of all types of armoured vehicles. Each battlegroup has an echelon or rear headquarters under the battalion or regimental quartermaster which is responsible for organising the distribution of supplies to the units of its battlegroup. At divisional level, its rear headquarters administers the movement of supplies to its brigades and battlegroups. Royal Corps of Transport and Royal Army Ordnance Corps assets are assigned to enable it to manage its supplies.

Armoured Engineers

Ever since the 79th Armoured Division's specialist tanks blasted through the German Atlantic Wall on D-Day, the British have always put great faith in armoured engineering vehicles and tactics. A whole family of specialist vehicles has been developed by the Royal Engineers to clear paths through minefields and field defences and breach anti-tank ditches. The

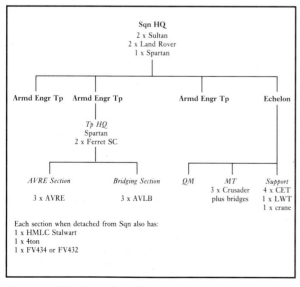

Armoured Engineer Squadron

FV-180 Combat Engineering Tractor (CET) is an amphibious tracked bulldozer vehicle designed to clear paths through earthworks under enemy fire and help prepare bridging sites. Armoured vehicle launched bridges (AVLB) are mounted on standard tank chassis and are used to place bridges over small water obstacles or anti-tank ditches. A key vehicle in the British armoured engineering inventory is the Armoured Vehicle Royal Engineers (AVRE), which is a converted Centurion tank. There are two main versions, one, the AVRE 165, has a 165 mm demolition gun which fires a 29 kg HESH round to destroy enemy bunkers or punch holes through earthworks. The AVRE 105 carries a standard 105 mm gun with special HESH demolition rounds. All AVREs are either fitted with a dozer blade or a mine plough and some can also carry fascines to fill in anti-tank ditches or rolls of metal trackways. The AVRE and CET can tow specialised trailers loaded with engineering stores or the Giant Viper mine clearing system. This is a rocket that pulls a tube of explosive behind it. Once the tube of explosives is astride the minefield it is detonated and the shock wave explodes any mines nearby. Friendly forces can then pass through the cleared area of the minefield.

Two types of units operate this equipment. 32 Armoured Engineer Regiment has three squadrons, which each muster some nine AVREs, nine AVLBs and four CETs. As the British Army adopted more mobile operations concepts during the 1980s it was decided that this capability should be available at lower levels of command. Close-support engineer squadrons were given trials during NATO exercises and they proved very successful. A squadron fielded three troops, each with two AVREs, two CETs and two AVLBs. The two armoured brigades that deployed to Saudi Arabia both took a close-support engineer squadron with them.

British all-arms doctrine calls for engineer support to be made available to brigades, battle groups and squadron/company groups depending on the task they are called on to perform. At all times the engineers would be supported by infantry, tanks and artillery to provide covering fire and allow for rapid exploitation of any breaches made in enemy defences. In defensive operations they also provide tank and infantry commanders with the ability to quickly dig anti-tank obstacles and field defences.

The massive anti-tank trenches dug by the Iraqi's to frustrate coalition armoured forces proved painfully inadequate in the face of vehicles such as the Chieftain AVLB bridge-layer. (MoD Army public relations)

FRENCH FORCES

French forces started to deploy to Saudi Arabia in September 1990 after Iraqi troops violated the diplomatic immunity of the French Embassy in Kuwait City and abducted three diplomats.

The ground elements of the force were all drawn from the 6th Light Armoured Division of the French Force d'Action Rapide, which is tasked to respond to threats to French interests outside Europe. Foreign Legionnaires from the 2ᵉ Regiment Etranger d'Infanterie and VAB armoured personnel carriers and 48 AMX-10RC light armoured fighting vehicles of the 1ᵉ Regiment Etranger de Cavalerie were shipped out to the Middle East on car ferries from Toulon to the Red Sea port of Yanbu. Engineers from the 6ᵉ Regiment Etranger de Genie were also deployed. A long land journey followed across the Arabian Peninsula to King Khalid Military City, where they co-operated with the main group of Arab forces until January, when they started to work with US forces.

For many years the French have led the way in the development of battlefield helicopter tactics and it was not surprising that elements of the 4th Airmobile Division should be included in the French contingent. Some 10 Puma transport helicopters and 32 HOT-armed Gazelle helicopters sailed from Toulon on the aircraft carrier *Clemenceau* for the Middle East before flying off to join the land contingent. They were supported by a 140 strong company from the 1ᵉ Regiment d'Infanterie.

In December 1990 further ground forces and

It was French troops such as these, equipped with their FAMAS rifles, that, alongside the British, launched the massive outflanking movement deep into southern Iraq which characterized the liberation of Kuwait. (Military Scene)

helicopters were dispatched to Saudi Arabia to boost the combat potential of the French contingent. Some 40 AMX-30B2 main battle tanks, of the 4^e Regiment Dragons, and 44 more AMX-10RCs proved a welcome addition as did some 50 more helicopters from the 4th Airmobile Division. By January 1990 13,300 French military personnel were deployed to the Middle East as part of Operation Daguet (Dagger) as the French effort was code-named.

The operational role was the subject of much controversy during the first months of the Gulf crisis because French forces in Saudi Arabia did not fully participate in joint exercises with the Americans and no heavy armour was deployed with the contingent that arrived in October. France's low-key approach to its military deployment had much to do with the political tight-rope being walked by President François Mitterand in his attempt to find a diplomatic solution to the crisis.

On the ground French soldiers trained hard to prepare themselves for the coming battle, and special forces contingents carried out deep reconnaissance missions into Iraq. These activities were revealed in October when a five-man patrol from the 13^e Regiment des Dragoons Parachutistes (a long-range recce unit) were captured inside Iraqi territory. They were handed over to the French Embassy in Baghdad by the Iraqis, who wanted to encourage French diplomatic activity.

ARAB COALITION FORCES

A significant percentage of the coalition forces were made up of a diverse collection of units from 12 Arab and Third World countries. Some provided important military assistance to the coalition while others could best be described as tokens of political support.

Saudi Arabia fielded a well-equipped array of ground forces from the kingdom's Army and National Guard. The Army's 4th, 8th and 20th Armoured Brigades and another brigade moved up to the Kuwaiti frontier early in the crisis to provide a first line of defence in front of US forces. A mechanised infantry brigade of the National Guard also moved up to the frontier region, along with units of the Army Airborne Brigade and Royal Saudi Marines.

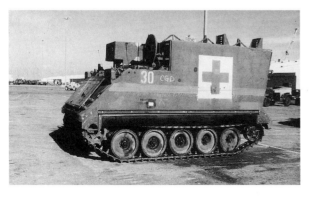

A vehicle which happily saw very little action in the Gulf War, this M577 ambulance stands on the dockside in Saudi Arabia still sporting its European colour scheme. (Military Scene)

The Saudi forces were equipped with some of the best military equipment oil dollars could buy, including French and American tanks, armoured vehicles, artillery, anti-tank missiles and small arms. A lack of manpower, however, meant that much of the Saudi arsenal had to be mothballed. In August 1990 an 8,000-strong Pakistani Brigade was despatched to Saudi Arabia to activate equipment positioned to defend the Kingdom's border with pro-Iraqi Yemen.

Units of the National Guard were some of the kingdom's best trained and equipped troops. This élite force evolved from Bedouin tribes who were known for their loyalty to the Saudi royal family, and have a key role in the kingdom's internal security forces.

Egypt provided the strongest military contingent to the coalition with some 35,000 troops being deployed to Saudi Arabia. The 3rd Mechanised Division and the 4th Armoured Division along with the 6th Armoured Brigade arrived in late 1990. The 5th Parachute Brigade completed the Egyptian contingent. Egyptian units operated a mix of Soviet and American equipment, including M113 APCs and 122 mm towed M1938 howitzers. A 400-600 strong parachute battalion was also based in the United Arab Emirates.

While Egyptian conscripts were best described as having variable fighting quality, Egyptian officers were some of the most experienced of the Arab coalition forces thanks to extensive training at Soviet and Western military academies and their combat experience during the 1973 Arab-Israeli war. The country's special forces and parachute units were also of a high quality; being professional soldiers, they also gained combat experience fighting on the Iraqi side during the 1980–88 Iran-Iraq war.

The coalition threw together some strange bed fellows and none was stranger than the involvement of Syria considering the country's previous strong pro-Soviet and anti-American stance. A 19,000-strong contingent was despatched to Saudi Arabia by Syrian President Assad between September and November 1990. A special forces regiment and the 9th Armoured Division equipped with some 200 T-62 and T-55 tanks formed the core of the Syrian contingent. They were fresh from fighting in Lebanon and were all highly trained professional soldiers. Some 500-600 paratroops were based in the United Arab Emirates.

Members of the Gulf Co-operation Council already had a brigade stationed in Saudi Arabia when the Iraqis invaded Kuwait. The brigade strength multi-national Peninsula Shield Force was based at the King Khalid Military City in north-eastern Saudi Arabia. It contained contingents from Qatar, Bahrain, Oman, Kuwait and the United Arab Emirates. By late December 1990 it mustered some 10,000

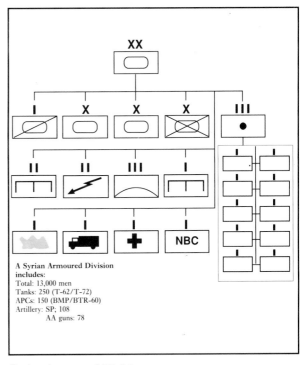

A Syrian Armoured Division includes:
Total: 13,000 men
Tanks: 250 (T-62/T-72)
APCs: 150 (BMP/BTR-60)
Artillery: SP; 108
AA guns: 78

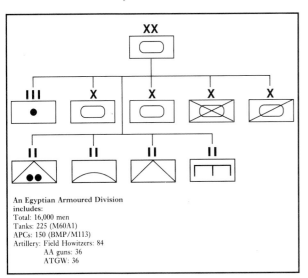

An Egyptian Armoured Division includes:
Total: 16,000 men
Tanks: 225 (M60A1)
APCs: 150 (BMP/M113)
Artillery: Field Howitzers: 84
AA guns: 36
ATGW: 36

Egyptian Armoured Division

Syrian Armoured Division

troops and a few hundred tanks and armoured vehicles.

Supporting the main Arab forces were a ragtag selection of light infantry forces, including 8,000 Bangladeshi troops in two brigades, 500 Senegalese, 500 soldiers from Niger and even a small band of Afghan Mujahadeen. Some 1,300 Moroccan motorised troops guarded the Assafaniya oil refinery complex. These contingents were of questionable military value but they provided welcome political support for the coalition. Cynics, however, put their participation down to the liberal distribution of Saudi oil dollars rather than commitment to the anti-Iraqi cause.

FREE KUWAITI FORCES

Some of the most highly motivated troops of the coalition were the Free Kuwaiti forces which escaped to Saudi Arabia after the Iraqi invasion. A large part of the 20,300-strong Kuwait armed forces were captured or destroyed during the August invasion, but the exiled Free Kuwaiti government used some of its $105 billion war chest to re-equip its depleted troops.

Elements of two brigades, some 7,000 troops, and a battalion of 50 British-built Chieftain main battle tanks escaped to Saudi Arabia. Dozens of Soviet-made BMP-2 infantry fighting vehicles also escaped with their crews after fighting rearguard actions through the streets of Kuwait city. A number of aircraft were flown to safety in Saudi Arabia and Bahrain, including eight Aerospatiale Gazelle helicopters fitted with HOT anti-tank guided missiles, one Puma transport helicopter, 19 A-4 Skyhawk fighter bombers and 15 Mirage F-1 fighters.

Much of the Kuwaiti arsenal fell into Iraqi hands. Many weapons, such as 24 Hawk surface-to-air missile systems, 36 M109 self-propelled 155 mm howitzers and 20 AMX Mk F-3 155 mm self-propelled howitzers, were integrated into the Iraqi army with technical help from Jordanian advisers.

The 35th Free Kuwaiti Brigade was re-built at Hafir al-Batin, drawing on escaped soldiers of the old army, new volunteers and soldiers serving abroad at

An Officer of the Free Kuwaiti Forces in Saudi Arabia. His grim expression and the badge on his battledress speak volumes about his thoughts on the invasion and systematic rape of his country by Iraq. (Military Scene)

the time of the Iraqi invasion. Spares were bought from the original manufacturers of the Kuwait equipment to keep the brigade's tanks and armoured vehicles operational and new stocks of ammunition were purchased. Some 300 M84 (T-72 derivatives) were ordered from Yugoslavia to re-equip the other Free Kuwaiti Brigade. During the liberation of Kuwait the Chieftain-equipped brigade was designated the Shid ('Martyr's') Brigade and the other formation was called the Fahah ('The Opening') Brigade.

Many members of the Kuwaiti armed forces opted to stay behind after the Iraqi invasion to lead groups of resistance fighters. In the confusion of the first days of occupation Kuwaiti police and military armouries were opened up. Weapons were distributed to the resistance before the Iraqis established firm control.

When the 5th US Special Forces Group arrived in Saudi Arabia in August 1990 it started to provide training and assistance to Kuwaiti resistance groups operating behind Iraqi lines. As well as harassing the Iraqi invaders, the resistance groups collected vital intelligence on Iraqi troop positions and protected Westerners hiding in Kuwait City.

COALITION HIGH COMMAND

Command arrangements for the coalition forces deployed in Saudi Arabia were built up over six months prior to the outbreak of war and reflect the delicate political make-up of the anti-Iraq coalition.

Nominally all forces in Saudi Arabia were under the command of the Kingdom's defence minister, Prince Khaled bin Sultan, but in reality US Central Command was the driving force behind coalition operations. A dual operational and political command arrangement operated to ensure all coalition forces were tactically co-ordinated, but political sensitivities were observed. At a political level the commanders of the various national contingents were based in Riyadh and they were the link with their respective governments.

Operational command was vested in Central Command at Riyadh under Gen. H. Norman Schwarzkopf. His air commander, Lt.Gen. Charles Horner, controlled all the coalition air forces and produced daily co-ordinated operational plans. The ground element of Central Command was the US 3rd Army under Lt.Gen. John Yeosock. Subordinated elements included the US VII and XVIII Corps, US Marine Amphibious Forces and Arab ground forces under Saudi command. French and British divisions were both eventually put under tactical command of US corps.

Gen. Schwarzkopf, known to his troops as 'stormin Norman' or 'The Bear', served a number of tours in Vietnam and was land commander during the US invasion of Grenada. He is a former commander of the 24th Infantry Division (Mechanised).

From family connections he is well experienced in the Middle East. Lieut.Gen. Yeosock also had plenty of experience of Saudi Arabia after serving as an advisors to the Saudi National Guard.

The Commander British Forces Middle East, Lt.Gen. Sir Peter de la Billiere, was an old Middle East hand. He served a number of times in the area during his time with the Special Air Service Regiment. He won the Military Cross in Oman in 1959 and speaks Arabic fluently. The commander of the 1st (British) Armoured Division, Maj.Gen. Rupert Smith, reported on operational matters to a US corps commander.

The overall French commander in the Middle East, Gen. Michel Roquejeoffre, like his British counterpart, was based in Riyadh. Gen. Jean-Charles Mouscardes, the commander of French ground forces until he was replaced because of illness by Gen. Bernard Janviers, operated from a forward headquarters with US forces.

Lt.Gen. Abdul Rahman, the Saudi land forces commander, commanded Egyptian, Syrian and other Arab forces operating in eastern Saudi Arabia. These forces worked closely with the US Marines in the area and had US artillery observers and forward air controllers attached.

NBC PROTECTION

British and United States Army units that deployed to Saudi Arabia were well equipped and trained to protect themselves from Iraqi chemical weapons. More than three decades of preparing to counter the Soviet chemical warfare threat in Europe had led to a wide range of protective suits, respirators (gas masks), decontamination, detection and warning equipment being developed by both countries.

The British equipment and defensive procedures were developed by the Nuclear, Chemical and Biological (NBC) centre at Winterbourne Gunner and the Chemical Warfare Establishment at Porton Down. They are regarded by experts as the best available and the United States Marine Corps, along with a number of Gulf states and Saudi Arabia,

A disturbing, but ultimately redundant necessity in the Gulf theatre, this NBC cell operating at a HQ shows a comfortingly low NBC level. The threat of Iraqi chemical weapons proved to be a paper Tiger. (MoD Army public relations)

quickly placed orders for large quantities of British NBC equipment in the weeks after the Iraqi invasion of Kuwait.

Each British serviceman is issued with what is termed NBC individual Protective Equipment (IPE), consisting of a charcoal-lined two-piece suit, rubber over-boots and gloves, an S-10 respirator, chemical detector paper and decontamination powder. The suits and respirator canisters have a finite life in chemically contaminated environments so servicemen are issued with spare suits and canisters. The S-10 has a drinking device so servicemen can drink from their water bottles without removing the respirator. Challenger tanks and other armoured vehicles are fitted with forced air systems to keep chemical agents outside of vehicles. Hand-held detectors called CAMs (Chemical Agent Monitor) are distributed to troops to help them locate chemical agents and NAIAD (Nerve Agent Immobilised Enzyme Alarm and Detector) warning devices can be sited around defensive positions to warn of chemical attacks.

At battalion, brigade and divisional headquarters special teams of officers and NCOs are assigned to NBC reporting cells to issue warnings of chemical attacks and monitor the level of contamination. Unlike the Soviets or Americans, the British do not have specialist decontamination vehicles to clear up after chemical attacks. Instead special bleaches and decontamination agents are applied by standard hoses or scrubbing brushes to vehicles, aircraft, stores, ground or personnel.

US NBC technology is considered not to be as advanced as British equipment. The American suits do not have an integral hood like the British suit so American GIs have to take their full hood off to change their respirator canister. M42 chemical alarm units are of an older vintage to the British NAIAD. All US armoured vehicles have filtration systems to protect their crews for chemical attack. The Americans termed their different levels of NBC alert states as Mission Orientated Protection Posture (MOPP).

US Army divisions each have a NBC company to train its soldiers in the use of NBC equipment, monitor contamination and operate special-purpose decontamination systems. They are also trained to plan the launching of chemical strikes by US chemical weapon delivery systems. Like British armoured reconnaissance units, US armoured cavalry units are trained to carry out reconnaissance of NBC contaminated areas. The capability of US units to conduct such missions was enhanced in October 1990 when the German Bundeswehr donated 30 Fuchs NBC reconnaissance vehicles to the US Army. A number of these very capable vehicles were also made available to British units in the Middle East.

While US Army units deployed to Saudi Arabia from Germany were well trained and equipped thanks to the ever present Soviet chemical threat, US Marine Corps units, which have primarily a Third World intervention role, were not so well equipped or trained and had to undergo a crash programme of NBC preparations when they arrived in Saudi Arabia in the autumn of 1990. A large quantity of the USMC's NBC equipment was also found to be obsolete or to have overrun its shelf life so new stocks had to be rapidly delivered to in-theatre units.

The coalition's chemical defence capability received a boost from an unexpected source when Czechoslovakia deployed a 185-man decontamination unit. It was flown out to Saudi Arabia by USAF C-5 Galaxy transport aircraft and was attached to the main Arab forces based around Hafir al-Batin.

SMART WEAPONS

Coalition forces in the Gulf were armed with some of

the world's most technologically advanced conventional weapons, which are known in popular jargon as 'smart' weapons. Thanks to recent advances in computer and laser systems this new generation of weapons are able to think for themselves and find their targets with remarkable accuracy.

The Copperhead 155 mm artillery round is guided to its target by a laser beam operated by ground troops or from a helicopter. It transforms standard artillery pieces from being relatively inaccurate area fire weapons into accurate tank killers. The helicopter-mounted Hellfire missile is also guided by laser beams. It is a 'fire and forget' missile which means the firing helicopter crew does not have to guide the missile to its target. The firing helicopter can then stay well out of sight or range of enemy anti-aircraft systems.

Laser target designators come in many shapes and sizes. Small systems can be carried by special forces teams and large long range systems are fitted to helicopters or aircraft. Once the target is illuminated by the laser, guided missiles or bombs fly down the laser beam on to the target. Sand storms, cloud or rain, however, can interrupt the laser beam and cause the guided weapon to go out of control.

Tank gunnery has been revolutionised by computers and lasers. Ballistic computers have made tank guns remarkably accurate. They calculate how weather conditions, barrel warp, propellant tempera-

ture and other crucial information affect gun accuracy to make sure a tank hits its target on the first shot, even when moving. Laser range finders have played a very important part in this revolution by giving ballistic computers vital information on the range of targets. Thermal imaging advances have also enabled Western-made tanks, such as the M1A1 and the Challenger, to fight just as well at night as in daylight.

A similar fire control system is fitted to the Multiple Launch Rocket System (MLRS) to enable targets to be engaged at up to 25 miles range with pinpoint accuracy. Computer navigation systems are used to allow MLRS crews to precisely chart their own locations and then calculate the firing data needed to put their rockets on target.

High technology has also been used to improve the destructive power of existing munitions. To defeat extra armour fitted to the latest generation Soviet tanks, such as the T-72, anti-tank missiles have been fitted with double warheads. The TOW-2 missile has a first-stage warhead that blows a path through a target's extra armour and the primary

A USMC LVTP sporting the Block I Appliqué Armour Kit (AAK) patrols along the Kuwaiti border. The additional armour is designed to defeat Rocket Propelled grenades and HEAT rounds. (Military Scene)

warhead then penetrates the main armour. Rocket Assisted Projectiles (RAP) are now standard in most US 155 mm howitzer batteries and they extend the gun's range by up to a third.

Iraq was also able to draw on Western high technology, thanks largely to the efforts of Western arms salesmen led by Dr. Gerald Bull. His Extended-Range, Full-Bore, Base-Bleed (ERFB-BB) ammunition when fired from his G-5 artillery system is able to hit targets up to 40 km away. The ammunition is fitted with a buring charge at the base of its shell that reduces drag during flight and hence increases the shell's range considerably. Soviet RAP rounds were also available for their Soviet-supplied artillery.

Laser range finders were also adapted by the Iraqis into anti-personnel weapons during the Iran-Iraq war. The modified laser range finders were used to sweep the ranks of massed Iranian infantry formation during 'human wave' attacks to cause eye injuries. Some 2,000 Iranians were reported to have suffered retinal injuries during several battles.

SATELLITE INTELLIGENCE

Coalition commanders in the Middle East had access to unprecedented intelligence on Iraqi military preparations thanks to special satellite terminals. US Army and US Marine Corps headquarters down to divisional level were all equipped with 'Constant Source' terminals which enabled them to plug straight into US photographic and electronic eavesdropping satellites orbiting over the Middle East. The terminals enabled commanders to receive printouts of satellite photographs and electronic data in their own headquarters. This information was made available to coalition allies.

The small terminals were easily transportable and allowed intelligence staffs to tailor the 'raw data' specifically to their own needs, for example by selecting photographic images relevant to their own

section of the battlefield. 'Constant Source' is part of a US programme called 'Tactical Employment of National Capabilities' which was established as a result of previous problems in getting vital intelligence information to field commanders. During the Vietnam War a special forces unit was sent to rescue US POWs from Son Tay POW camp, but satellite information received days before the mission showed that the POWs had been moved. The rescue party only discovered this fact when they fought their way into the prison camp and found it was empty.

There were three KH-11 photographic reconnaissance satellites, a Lacrosse radar satellite and two electronic 'ferret' satellites over the Middle East. Lacrosse satellites map terrain and are ideal for spotting ships and large structures such as bridges. Ferret satellites were able to locate the positions of radars, command posts and other military equipment that emitted electronic signals. Photographic and radar satellites, however, were not a panacea for intelligence problems because their orbits meant they were only over Iraq and Kuwait for a few hours a day. This prevented the supply of realtime intelligence needed for fast-moving armoured battle.

Electronic eavesdropping by satellites and ground stations was a more reliable source of information about what was happening behind Iraqi lines. Each US corps, division and brigade contained a military intelligence unit to keep track of enemy electronic emissions. Photographic reconnaissance aircraft were useful, but they also suffered from

A group of squaddies take a break at Al Jubail West service station. The second figure from the left quenches his thirst with a can of alcohol-free beer. (Military Scene)

This Humvee of the US Marine Corps Military Police (note the blue light) has a formidable box-fed M60 machine gun mounted in the anti-aircraft role. (US DoD via Tim Ripley)

problems over time-lag between the photographs being taken and the film being returned to base for processing.

For realtime intelligence, remotely piloted vehicles (RPV) proved to be a great advance. Most British and US target locating units were equipped with these useful systems. RPVs are very small remotely controlled aircraft that are fitted with television cameras. Their function is to fly over enemy lines and send back realtime television images of the current situation. The Israelis used them to great effect during the 1982 Israeli invasion of Lebanon when they located Syrian surface-to-air missile sites. Israeli controllers were then able to target air and artillery strikes on to the missiles.

THE COALITION COUNTER ATTACK

After months of careful preparation and planning the coalition launched their campaign to liberate Kuwait with massive air strikes against strategic targets throughout Iraq in the early hours of 17 January 1991. A wide range of targets were hit in the coalition's campaign to destroy Iraq's command and control system, air force and weapons of mass destruction.

While Iraq's strategic infrastructure was being demolished, coalition ground forces moved up to their jumping-off points near Kuwait in preparation for the ground offensive.

In a propaganda ploy President Saddam Hussein launched a series of spoiling attacks against Saudi Arabia at the end of January. Most of these were dealt with by US Marine anti-armour units, but on 30 January a brigade of the 3rd Iraqi Mechanised Division advanced into the undefended Saudi border town of Khafji. Heavy fighting followed as the Saudi 8th National Guard Battalion, supported by Qatari troops and US Marine AH-1W Cobra gunships, drove out the Iraqis with the loss of more than 100 tanks and armoured vehicles.

Increasing coalition tactical air strikes and artillery fire was now brought down on the Iraqi frontline positions in preparation for the ground offensive.

Within hours of the coalition's 22 February deadline to withdraw from Kuwait the ground offensive began. American, British, French, Saudi, Egyptian, Syrian, Qatari, Omani and Free Kuwait troops advanced north against the Iraqis. Arab forces and US Marines took on the main Iraqi defences in front of Kuwait. The US Army heavy armour, British and French units mounted a massive outflanking manoeuvre through the desert to the west of Kuwait. They swept north into Iraq and then swung

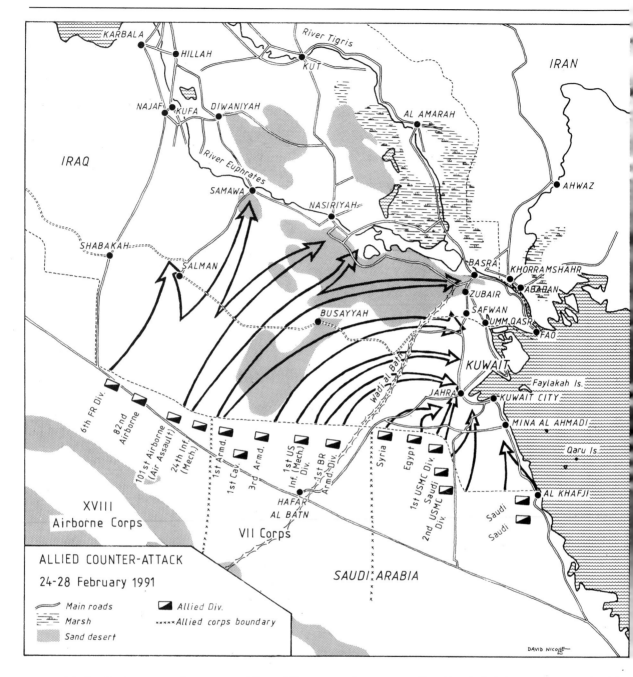

KARBALA

HILLAH

River Tigris

KUT

IRAN

NAJAF KUFA DIWANIYAH

AL AMARAH

River Euphrates

IRAQ

SAMAWA

NASIRIYAH

AHWAZ

SHABAKAH

SALMAN

BASRA

KHORRAMSHAHR

ZUBAIR

ABADAN

SAFWAN

BUSAYYAH

UMM QASR

FAO

KUWAIT

Wadi al Batn

Faylakah Is.

JAHRA

KUWAIT CITY

MINA AL AHMADI

Qaru Is.

6th FR Div.

82nd Airborne

101st Airborne (Air Assault)

24th Inf. (Mech.)

1st Armd.

1st Cav.

3rd Armd.

1st US Inf. (Mech.) Div.

1st BR Armd. Div.

Syria

Egypt

1st USMC Div.

2nd USMC Div.

Saudi Saudi

AL KHAFJI

Saudi Saudi

XVIII
Airborne Corps

HAFAR
AL BATN

VII Corps

SAUDI ARABIA

ALLIED COUNTER-ATTACK

24-28 February 1991

〰 Main roads   ◣ Allied Div.

▦ Marsh   ×××× Allied corps boundary

▒ Sand desert

DAVID NICOLLE

east to hit the Iraq armoured reserve and Republican Guard in the flank.

All along the front, Iraqi morale collapsed under the weight of coalition firepower. More than 200,000 Iraqis surrendered and up to 100,000 were killed or wounded in the rout. Coalition forces suffered under 100 fatalities and a similar number of wounded. In total some 41 of 42 Iraqi divisions were smashed in 100 hours of ground fighting.

By 25 February Kuwait was liberated and US President George Bush declared a ceasefire on 27 February. Coalition forces, however, had already stopped fighting – there were no Iraqi troops left to engage.